SHOWING UP
FOR LIFE

About the book:

A true account of the writer's emergence from compulsive overeating, *Showing Up For Life* looks beyond diets. It openly describes the emotional and spiritual transformation that rehabilitated her body and soul, allowing her to lose over 160 pounds. The isolation and double life of food obsession are tenderly revealed, showing how compulsive eaters' use of food limits and controls their world. *Showing Up For Life* probes the reasons Heidi Waldrop began to depend on food for security and comfort as well as the realization that brought her to a place where she could give up her addiction and face life squarely without a numbing substance. The process of a heart in transition is felt in the pages, as Heidi recounts the emotional and social changes she faced in giving up her addiction and living at a normal weight after being obese most of her life. Freed from the compulsion to overeat, she began to resolve complex intimacy issues and discover a deeper richness in life.

About the author:

Heidi Waldrop was an intern for *Family Circle* and worked on staff at various McGraw-Hill magazines, such as *Business-Week*, before becoming a free-lance writer in 1982. Since then she has written hundreds of articles, particularly in the travel field, for magazines such as *McCall's*, *Travel & Leisure*, and *Working Woman*.

SHOWING UP FOR LIFE

A Recovering Overeater's Triumph Over Compulsion

Heidi Waldrop

 HAZELDEN®

First published October 1990.

ISBN: 0-89486-714-8
Library of Congress Catalog Number: 90-81780

Printed in the United States of America.

Editor's note:

Hazelden Educational Materials offers a variety of information on chemical dependency and related areas. Our publications do not necessarily represent Hazelden or its programs, nor do they officially speak for any Twelve Step organization.

The stories in this book are true. In most cases, names of the people involved have been changed to protect their anonymity.

The Twelve Steps of Alcoholics Anonymous, printed at the back of this book, is reprinted with permission of Alcoholics Anonymous World Services, Inc. Permission to reprint the Twelve Steps of A.A. does not mean that A.A. has reviewed or approved the contents of this publication, nor that A.A. agrees with the views expressed herein. A.A. is a program of recovery from alcoholism. Use of the Twelve Steps in connection with programs which are patterned after A.A. but which address other problems does not imply otherwise.

Contents

This book is dedicated to my parents, who taught me the fundamental principles of God that I came home to in recovery, and to Jeffrey, whose openness to growth and loving support have helped me to fly.

For helping me make this book possible, I thank God, Faith Childs, Patrick Lane, Shawn Hancock, Dale Thompson, Deb Cooperman, my Seattle book club, Joyce Klimoski, and all those gentle, strong souls who have been examples to me in recovery.

Prologue

Upon awakening one sunny morning in September 1985, my first awareness was nausea. Rolling on my side, I used both hands to heave my three hundred-pound body to a sitting position on the edge of the bed. That's when my eyes fell on the half-eaten chocolate cake, scattering of cookies, and empty Doritos bag on the table across the room of my studio apartment. Not again, I thought.

I shut my eyes against the image of the night before, but it still remained: Standing unnoticed at the door of a cocktail party for magazine editors and writers, I had panicked to see a room full of slim, confident people, only a few of whom I knew. Fear swamped me. I suddenly felt that the black-and-red-checked dress I'd sewn looked juvenile on my massive frame. The articles I had published as a free-lance magazine writer didn't seem good enough to me, and the magazines they were published in seemed second-rate. Backing slowly out the door, I grabbed my coat and left. Just get me home, I pleaded as I frantically waved down a taxi.

Uncontrollable, hateful feelings about my body, my life, and myself poured through me as I entered my apartment and heard the phone ringing.

It was Steve calling to see if I was still going to join him and a small group of friends for a movie that night. My heart jumped at the sound of his voice. We'd been friends for a few months now, but I longed to be more than friends. Thinking about the night ahead, I started feeling depressed. Remember Heidi, we're just friends, I told myself. Knowing that he cared about me didn't halt the feeling spiraling downward inside me. Of course we're just friends, I thought bitterly. As I sat on the couch, my glance locked on my stomach with Buddha-like ripples of fat. You're *fat*. He'd never consider you romantically. Something slammed shut inside me. Not tonight. After the horror of the cocktail party, I couldn't deal with feeling inadequate and with competing with two other women for his attention. The image of me eating pizza in front of the television suddenly filled my mind, blocking Steve's words and pointing me to my escape, my safe place.

I interrupted him. "Listen Steve, I don't think I can make it tonight. I've got this article to finish that I have to turn in to *McCall's* first thing tomorrow." I hoped I sounded disappointed, as though my life as a magazine writer in New York was so exciting and demanding that it couldn't be put off.

As I got off the phone, a jab of loss hit me. Then fear. What if he doesn't call again? It was the third time I had pulled out of plans in the last month, always pleading some pressing deadline. I can't help it if my career is so pressured, I thought defensively. That's the price of success in the Big Apple. If my friends can't handle it, tough.

Within an hour I had finished the article and ordered a pizza to be delivered. It was still early. I could call Steve back to go to the movie, I thought halfheartedly. But the idea of my safe cocoon-like evening had already supplanted any desire to be out with people. Later, as I ate the pizza, I pictured the group out together, talking and laughing, and felt cheated. I dropped the piece of pizza I'd been eating back in the box and jammed the box into the refrigerator.

The knot in my stomach was twisting tighter by the moment. I had to find something to loosen it. I picked up the phone and dialed my oldest sister, Amanda, who lives in Texas. "Hi, it's Heidi," I said in a light tone, wondering why I had called her and what I was going to say.

"Heidi! It's good to hear from you. How are you?"

I couldn't tell her I felt cold and apathetic, so distant from everything and everyone that it frightened me. After all, what could she do about it? "Not so great," I finally squeaked out, telling her I was worried about money. Cash flow was always so uncertain for a free-lance writer.

"Heidi, I'm so sorry things aren't going well. Do you think there is a way you could make more money? Or at least have things more stable by working on staff at a magazine?" she asked.

I didn't want help figuring out answers to my problems. I suddenly felt edgy and regretted opening up. I didn't want her, or anyone, to be that close — to know how lonely, insecure, and frightened I really was. The image of success I'd always presented to my three married sisters was slipping. She probably felt sorry for poor, single Heidi.

She isn't really listening to me, I thought with annoyance as I shifted the phone to my other ear. How could she understand anyway? She has five kids and doesn't have a career. Suddenly I wanted to get off the phone. "Listen, I'm fine, really, I'm just tired. I better get back to work," I lied, as I hung up the phone.

I paced the floor. What did you want from her anyway, Heidi? To fix you? I chided myself derisively as if verbally slapping some adolescent into shape. The thought that I would be that needy, that I couldn't be whole on my own, repelled me. Then some defense withered inside, and I felt a sharp ache. Yes, I thought, as I melted onto my familiar couch. I want somebody to come in and rescue me. But nobody came.

Looking at the clock I noticed it was only 8:30. Too early to go to bed. I'll go for a walk and get some fresh air, I thought and headed along Second Avenue, making it only as far as the deli. Picking chocolate cake, some Häagen-Dazs ice cream, and a half dozen candy bars, I headed home.

Back in the apartment, I opened the ice cream and a jar of peanut butter, set them on the table, and alternated bites until the ice cream was gone. It wasn't until I'd finished that I realized I was still in my coat. Easing out of my coat, I flipped on the television, and cut a piece of cake. At the commercial break I sliced another small piece, and by the end of the hour-long show half the cake was gone. Now, I thought, I want something different, something salty and crunchy.

As I settled in to watch the next show, I grabbed the bag of Doritos and tub of onion dip. Pulling out one large, perfect chip, I poked it into the tub so the edges were evenly rimmed with the creamy dip. Plucking another chip, I repeated the procedure until the entire bag was empty. My mind began to roam the contents of the cupboard even as I put the remnants of the dip in the fridge. There was a tin of nuts, the new package of doughnuts, a couple of Hostess fruit pies, a half-full bag of pretzels, and an unopened package of Oreos. That's what I want, Oreos. I hummed to myself as I pulled the package out and headed back to the couch. I was getting more and more drugged on sugar.

A half hour later I was determinedly stuffing my second candy bar down when I noticed it was 10:30. Time for bed, I thought as I got up from the couch. My brain was blank. I could hardly remember why I'd been so upset earlier. But it all came back to me when I lifted the lid of the trash can and saw the yawning ice cream carton. Loneliness, misery, and confusion flooded over me. Those feelings were quickly replaced by a spreading panic. What am I doing? Why can't I stop? I wondered. Thinking about tomorrow, I saw no reason for it to be any different than today.

Turning away in disgust, I dressed for bed. I was able to avoid my image until, vigorously brushing my teeth free of the remnants of food, I inadvertently glanced in the bathroom mirror.

My eyes locked on the distorted, bloated face looking back at me. Who is that, and what has she done to herself? I thought distantly. In the stillness of the night, all I could do was look back at the image that was supposed to be me, entranced by the bleary-eyed, puzzled stare.

                      ❧ ❧ ❧ ❧ ❧

    I spent most of my adult life caught in the grips of an addiction to a deceptively innocuous substance — food. Overweight from the time I was twelve years old, I grew to weigh 330 pounds by the time I was twenty-nine. I was sure that if I just found the right diet and lost weight, my life would be filled with laughter and happiness. I focused on the next miracle diet — liquid protein, Weight Watchers, Diet Center, eating only one meal a day, eating certain combinations of food — until there were no more. Then I descended into hopelessness. It became increasingly difficult just to live life, my body twice the size of an average woman's, and my soul consumed with fear and anxiety. But in August 1986, I discovered I was suffering from compulsive overeating, an illness similar to alcoholism. It was a hard realization: I didn't want to face the idea that I ate uncontrollably, eating to escape my feelings just as alcoholics drink uncontrollably to escape theirs.

    But in facing that awful reality, not only did I see others who had been able to recover from compulsive overeating, I began to believe that I, too, could move away from the horror that was my daily reality. Through a Twelve Step program of recovery for compulsive overeaters based on Alcoholics Anonymous,* I've been able to lose 160 pounds, wear shorts,

---

* See the Twelve Steps of Alcoholics Anonymous at the end of this book.

and take part in sports with friends rather than sitting on the sidelines. But, most importantly, I now feel comfortable in my own skin and am rid of the constant knot of anxiety that twisted in my stomach. I'm not afraid that people will discover the "bad" person I thought I had inside me and leave me. I can enjoy being who I am today, unencumbered by past anger and future fears. This book is about the process that is transforming both my body and my soul — enabling me to live rather than merely survive, to have choices, and to *feel* without a sugar anesthetic.

CHAPTER ONE

Growing Up

Ever since I can remember I ate to find a sense of calm or to feel safe. I grew up in a quiet neighborhood in Oklahoma City, as the fourth of seven children in a very religious family. Between the seven of us and our various foster siblings, there was always some sort of trauma in progress in our home.

When I was born in July 1956, Amanda, my oldest sister, was four years old, and my next oldest sister, Joanne, was soon to turn three. But everyone's focus at that time was on Thomas. At twenty-one months, he was a mystery to my parents. He couldn't talk and seemed slower than other babies his age. While my father focused on establishing his career in orthopedic surgery, often being called to the emergency room in the middle of the night or during some family gathering, Mother struggled to keep our growing brood together. It was increasingly difficult for my parents to cope. Their time in those first few years after I was born was consumed with carting Thomas from one doctor to another until, finally, the conclusion was reached that he was irreversibly brain damaged.

Three more children rounded out our family over the next several years. Lisa, all giggles and smiles, came along four years after me. Michael, an exact, stocky, no-nonsense duplicate of my father, arrived a year later. Then, as Michael turned five, our family adopted Daniel, a shy, confused three-year-old who had been adopted before. My parents hoped that the two younger boys would become companions.

Soon after I was born, as my parents did their best to put out whatever fire was hottest and continued to keep Thomas in our home, my mother's mother came to live with us. Mimi, as we called her, became my mother and protector, my source of nurturing and joy. When I was four, she moved to a duplex apartment a few blocks away, and there I spent weekends ensconced in comfort and appreciation. Stepping out of the chaos of home, where I felt lost in a crowd, I came to a place where I was special.

Arriving one late Friday afternoon the spring before I turned eight, I found Mimi in the kitchen. She looked so proper, wearing — as always — silk stockings and a dress. Looking down to see me, her face melted into a smile full of love, and her tall, slim frame softened to envelope me in a hug. "How about some chocolate chip ice cream?" she asked, still holding me close, but pulling back a bit to see my reaction. Nodding vigorously, I could already picture the round tub with the window on top revealing big chocolate chips in white ice cream.

Sitting on the back step a few minutes later, we ate our ice cream as Mimi asked me how piano lessons were going. My face lit up. "My teacher and I played on two big pianos next to each other today. We're going to play a two-piano duet in my recital next month." I spooned a heaping mound of ice cream into my mouth. "I'm going to have to practice real hard, but it will be great. I'm the only one who gets to play the duet with Mr. Stone."

Finishing our ice cream, we cuddled as we watched streaks of orange fade with the setting sun. As the sky grew dark, we went back inside and to the bedroom closet. "Which one will it be tonight?" Mimi asked, as she pulled out a box filled with wonderful smelling packages of bubble bath. I chose my favorite, the one that smelled of roses. After my bath, I curled up under mounds of blankets in my poster bed next to Mimi's, and we held hands on the night stand between our beds until I fell asleep.

Though Mimi's nurturance was my lifeline, it became a source of deep hostility between me and my father and sisters. "Listen, Heidi goes over to your mother's house more often than any of the other kids," I heard my father say to my mother as I walked down the hall a few nights later. I stopped midstep to listen. Joanne had been complaining to Dad the night before that Mimi didn't like her and that I got special treatment. Now I was afraid they wouldn't let me go to Mimi's as much. "She's so protective of Heidi and pampers her too much," Dad continued. "Heidi needs to learn to do things on her own. She'll never make much of herself if your mother keeps doing things for her."

Mother had an exasperated edge in her voice when she responded. "Bob, with two kids in diapers and me having to watch Thomas twenty-four hours a day so he doesn't tear the house apart, what else can I do? It's a relief for me to have my mother take Heidi," she said. "Besides, you know they have a special relationship." I was filled with mixed emotions as I turned away and walked upstairs. I hated being in the middle of a fight between my parents. Why wouldn't Dad just leave me alone? I wondered angrily. I knew he didn't like Mimi, and now I sensed he didn't like me either.

❦ ❦ ❦ ❦ ❦

Although we lived in a rambling old house downtown, Dad loved being out in the country. So on Saturdays, except when it was snowing or freezing, most of us would troop out to our farm on the edge of the city. Here, Dad introduced us to the delights of a farm as he remembered them from growing up in rural Texas. I didn't take much to the cattle or tractors, but horses went straight to my heart.

One Saturday morning the summer I turned ten, the sun had barely risen when I was trailing along behind my father and Amanda as we headed through the pastures into our horses' favorite corner. I had trouble keeping up with Dad and Amanda as they walked a few feet ahead with their heads bent together, deep in conversation. Amanda's long blonde hair lifted with the breeze as she turned her head and laughed, recounting to Dad the antics at a play rehearsal the day before. As my father pointed out something on the horizon, I ran a few steps to catch up, but I couldn't reach them. Then I saw for myself: Golden Prince, Bay Girl, and Red Dandy raised their heads and whinnied as we approached.

My heart turned over at the sight of my Red Dandy. My passion for horses was sparked the moment I had sat precariously on a pony when I was four, and had only deepened when the spirited little chestnut colt had been born three years later. He unofficially became my horse, and there he was now, trotting alongside Golden Prince in the far field. We walked up to the three horses slowly, in a practiced motion that allowed us to form a net that edged them into the corner fence line. Slipping their halters on, we led them back to the barn to saddle them. Within a few minutes I was in ecstasy as I rode Dandy. Amanda continued talking with Dad as they rode their horses. Then, in a break, he turned back to me. "Shall we all gallop?" he asked. My vigorous nod and grin affirmed the obvious answer. Putting my head on Dandy's neck, I whispered, "Let's go, buddy," and we all took off. The sun was strong on my back as we flew through the fields. Nothing existed but the feeling of flying, as though I were one with the power and freedom of the sturdy little horse beneath me.

の の の の の

Woven underneath the image of a typical large family full of love was a thread of compulsion and overeating, which our parents, and then some of us kids, used to dull painful feelings. We were served simple meat-and-potatoes meals, usually rather late because Dad was kept at the hospital emergency room, and the food frequently burned because mother was often distracted by the children and her household responsibilities. As haphazard as our eating appeared on the surface, the deeper, secret message was that food was compelling in its enticements. I knew where the "drug" was if I wanted it. Candy and nuts always littered my father's dresser drawers. Cookies were hidden behind the Tupperware on the top shelf of the kitchen cabinet, or in the closet in Dad's study. The funny thing was that the hiding places weren't secret; we all knew where they were.

Dad's case of favorite scotch in the closet had given way to a stash of candy when he quit drinking for religious reasons soon after my parents were married. Because he worked obsessively as a physician eighteen hours a day and got intense exercise on the farm, he wasn't overweight. He presented a portrait of a dashing, dark-haired doctor. By the time I was ten I had taken on Dad's Depression-era fear of never having enough. I felt the need to "binge while the sun shines," grabbing and hoarding large quantities of food to eat later. Sometimes I'd take money from mother's wallet and buy candy bars that I hid in my room. Other times I'd put a handful of cookies in a plastic bag in my closet to eat before I went to bed.

Mother ate compulsively as far back as I can remember, although it was rarely in large quantities. She "grazed," picking at chips or cookies throughout the day. Mother had only gained a few pounds with her various pregnancies and looked only slightly matronly with her fine-boned features and curly chestnut-brown hair. Over the years I picked up mother's attitude about food, offering to fix dinner so I could pick at whatever I wanted while I cooked.

By the autumn of my tenth year, food had subconsciously become a tool I used to express a variety of emotions from effusive love to submerged anger. One night I was playing with my Barbie dolls in the living room when my father stuck his head around the corner. "Heidi, how about we all head out for root beer floats?" he said with a grin. Sweeping me up off the floor to tickle me, he carried me to the hall as he yelled to the other kids; then we headed to the car. While we waited for the others to come, Dad pulled a package of cookies out from under the seat in the car. "Want some?" he asked, handing me two. We munched in silent camaraderie for a few seconds before the other kids descended on us.

Just a few nights later Dad arrived home from the hospital, looking weary and exasperated as Mother directed us to put the overcooked food on the table. I sat down in my chair, still fuming about the night before. Dad had been an hour late for my piano recital because he was at the hospital, as usual, and missed seeing me perform entirely. He hadn't even said he was sorry and had probably already forgotten. On top of that, Mother had been so preoccupied with the little kids she hadn't seen me either.

"Eat your vegetables, Heidi," mother said now, looking up from where she was feeding Daniel. I was startled. It was the first thing she'd said to me in hours.

"I don't want them. I'm full," I replied, defiantly tilting my chin.

Just then Dad came back to the table from stopping a fight between the boys. He looked ready to explode. "Stuff the junk down, Heidi," he said, in exasperated distraction. When I didn't, he grabbed my arm and, in one swift motion, hauled me out of the chair and to my bedroom for a sound spanking. As my father closed the door, I slowly lay down on the bed. He still hadn't said he was sorry about my recital. Tears slid down my burning face.

Typical confusion was all I felt a few weeks later as the family sat down for Thanksgiving dinner — finally. The whirlwind was in full motion when my father arrived from the hospital and began carving the turkey. Thomas was home from boarding school, and Amanda's energy was fully monopolized in keeping food going into his mouth and not on everyone else. Mother was looking for the gravy ladle and couldn't find it.

Instead she found two empty cookie packages. "Joanne," she called automatically in a tone of disgust.

"What, Mom?" Joanne responded from upstairs.

"Get down here," was Mother's reply.

At thirteen, Joanne was thirty pounds overweight and the one in the family with "the weight problem." "Did you eat these?" Mother asked now, as Amanda unobtrusively slipped out of the room without being questioned.

Joanne, looking guilty, also looked straight at me. "Heidi ate some of them," she said. Horrified, I wondered if Joanne had seen me eating the handful I had grabbed after dinner the night before or if she was just guessing.

Exasperated, Mother pointed at Joanne's tight pants. "Whether Heidi ate any or not, you can't go on eating like this," she said. "It would help if you would get some exercise and stick with the tennis lessons I arranged for you. Now go get washed for dinner and help Amanda with Thomas."

Turning to me as Joanne went back upstairs, Mother said, "Heidi, you don't want to have a weight problem like Joanne, do you? You've gained a few pounds lately. We'll have to watch more what you eat. No more sweets."

≈ ≈ ≈ ≈ ≈

By the next Thanksgiving, when I was eleven, Mimi had died, and everything had changed, especially my self-image. Food, or more precisely fat, had become an issue in my life. One afternoon, dressed in black leotards and pink tights, my best friend, Ann, and I giggled and stretched before ballet class began. Ann and I had been dipping and swirling together at Ingram's Ballet School two afternoons a week since I was five. I found a cherished part of myself in that magical world of grace, feeling beautiful each spring when we put on delicate pastel costumes and performed on stage in the high school auditorium. Now, Ann and I were talking about our latest crush. Looking around as we talked, I thought how I loved the room, with its smell of polished wood and its line of mirrors that seemed to go on eternally.

"Chop, chop, girls. Let's begin now," Mrs. Ingram said as the pianist began the precise march that told us class was underway. A few minutes later, as I finished a series of turns across the floor, I caught my reflection in the mirror. My legs looked chunky next to Ann's. Pausing to look again, I saw in my mind the image of Mother, the night before, wagging her finger at Joanne. A vague, yet growing uneasiness and embarrassment built inside of me. I hadn't really ever compared my body with anyone else's before. I can't be fat, I thought, hurrying to get in line next to Julia to compare our sizes. I'm bigger, I realized with a start. Upset, I got in line by Elaine on the next series of turns. She was the biggest in the class . . . I thought. But we didn't look much different, did we? I couldn't tell. Was I larger or smaller? I suddenly felt like an elephant where moments before I'd felt like a lithe gazelle.

As Ann and I walked out of class, I wanted to ask if she thought I was fat, but stopped myself when I remembered her recent remark about how fat Elaine looked in a leotard. I kept expecting her to look at me with the same disgust that had twisted her face when she made the comment about Elaine. Suddenly I wanted a candy bar. I suggested we go across the street to the store for a snack while we waited for Mother to pick us up. We roamed the aisles, and as Ann picked up one candy bar, I came around the corner with four, plus a cupcake.

"Are you going to eat all those?" she asked, horrified.

"Oh, no, I'm taking some candy home to Lisa, Michael, and Daniel," I replied quickly.

"Oh, then let's get some more cupcakes for them too," she said. I followed her, shocked at how easily I had just lied. I didn't want her to know they were all for me.

From then on I realized I couldn't eat what I really wanted around other people. By the spring when I was eleven, having gained fifteen extra pounds, I made the first of scores of visits to Weight Watchers. Mother began to monitor, and comment on, everything I ate. While she cooked special meals for Joanne and me, and cut sweets out of our diet, I couldn't stop myself from sneaking candy when she wasn't around.

Puberty hit me and my friends full force the autumn of seventh grade, and fat became even more of an issue for me. I had been part of the in crowd in sixth grade. Ann and I organized parties on weekend nights at her house or mine, and I had found my role, next to Ann, as the party-giver. But as we entered junior high school our tight little group split up when Ann and some of the others went to a private Catholic school. Only I and a few of my friends went to Harding Junior High.

The first couple of months of seventh grade, Ann and I tried to have parties like before, but everybody was talking about their own school. One night in October I realized things would never be the same again. As I came in the door of Craig's house I saw our old crowd, but there were almost as many new faces as old. Who were all these other people? I wondered, annoyed that Craig hadn't just stuck with our old crowd. Two thin, pretty girls I didn't recognize seemed to look down their noses at me as I edged into the kitchen to drop off the potato chips I'd brought.

"Who are those girls?" I asked Ann a couple of minutes later. "Oh, Jacqui and Brenda, the *really* cool girls at my school. I can't believe they came to our party. Isn't it great?"

Yeah, great, I thought as I moved back into the main room. I'm cool too. Why can't those girls figure that out? I didn't know how to tell them or show them. Perching on the edge of a chair, I thought of the days in grade school when all my pals surrounded me.

When it came time for spin the bottle and other kissing games, which we often played in the basement of my house at other parties, I withdrew to the edge of the room rather than running the game like I usually did. I wasn't sure the new guys would want to kiss me. Suppose one of them made a scene about it? I couldn't stand the thought of it. Some people had left early, so when everyone had paired up for kissing games, I was left over. I quickly looked to see if anyone had noticed. They hadn't, so I immediately busied myself with cleaning up after the party, picking at the leftover cake.

I had already cut an extra piece of cake and wrapped it to carry home when I remembered with horror the day before. Mother had found empty Reese's peanut butter cup wrappers in my underwear drawer. She came straight to where I sat in the family room, waving the wrappers in front of my face energetically. "If you keep eating this way you'll be as big as a house," she said. "You'll never be happy until you lose weight. No man will ever marry you." Then as an afterthought she asked, "Where did you get the money to buy these anyway?" I cringed. I'd taken the money from her wallet on the way to school that day. What could I say? My mind frantically sought a plausible answer. Luckily, just then a fight broke out between Joanne and Lisa, and Mother turned to settle it. I was off the hook, at least for now.

Later that night I watched as Mother pulled an apple pie out of the cupboard behind the Tupperware and cut a sliver as she prepared dinner. The pie sat on the counter over the next couple of hours, diminishing by half as she stopped to absently cut tiny pieces to eat between cleaning projects. At dinner, which was late because we waited for Dad to come home from the hospital, I hardly ate anything. Then, after everyone went to bed, I slipped downstairs. All I found in the sweets cupboard was hard candy, so I crept into Dad's den closet where I knew he kept his stash. Nothing. Darn it, I thought, until I remembered the cookies usually hidden under the seat of his car. Padding out the back door in my slippers, I found what I wanted in the car.

Now as I finished cleaning up Craig's kitchen after the party, I unwrapped the cake. If I wanted it, I'd have to eat it right now or find a better hiding place in my bedroom.

಄ ಄ ಄ ಄ ಄

In late September, while dancing in a church youth program, I strained my left knee. Several girls about my age — all of them thin — had been doing the cancan. In trying to keep up, I had kicked too high and fallen. By mid-October my knee hurt whenever I bent it or put weight on it, especially when I had to walk up and down the stairs in my four-story school. After awhile it began to give way unexpectedly as I climbed the stairs. My mother took me to see a doctor, who told me I needed to stay off it for a few weeks.

One Thursday morning in November I woke feeling the same jabbing pain in my knee that had kept me home since Monday.

My leg did feel a little better than it had, though, and I wondered if I should just make myself go. My stomach clutched at the thought of having to face my friends and explain that I had been absent because of my knee again. And I hated hobbling up the stairs with everyone watching and wondering what the big thing was that encased my knee. I'd have to explain that it was a splint to support my knee so I could walk. I closed my eyes, trying to push away the memory of how the splint drew more attention to my bulky frame. Instead, my thoughts were drawn to the day before. When I had told Mother my knee was hurting again, she had waved me to the couch and told me to stay home. I'd gathered some cookies and a pillow and spent the day reading a romance novel.

My mental tug-of-war continued. Would I stay home or wouldn't I? Mother was so busy, she wouldn't notice or care. She wouldn't push me one way or another. She was too overwhelmed with the other children. This week Thomas was being moved from a private home to a large dormitory-like school where he could get special educational care.

Besides, both my parents were focused on getting Joanne, now sixteen, to straighten up. The night before mother had discovered empty beer bottles in the trunk of her car. I had been in the den watching television when mother called upstairs to Joanne in the same disgusted tone I'd heard her use many times when talking to Joanne about food or some other part of her behavior. Only this time my father was at her side. They took Joanne into the living room and closed the door.

A couple of hours later Dad came into the den. "What's all this about your knee hurting?" he asked as he sat on the edge of the couch. I immediately felt wary. Why did he want to know? Was he going to push me to do something I didn't want to do? I'd heard him tell Joanne a few nights earlier that he thought that I just needed to be pushed, that I needed to toughen up. Well, I don't trust him, I thought defensively. We never talked unless he was teaching me a life lesson or questioning me about why I was doing something.

"Here, let me examine your knee again," he said. Although I sensed he was trying to be friendly, I just sat there letting him move it around and responding with yes and no to his attempts at conversation.

"Well," he said finally, "I think we're looking in the wrong place. It isn't the knee joint, but maybe the ligaments. Let's get you to Dr. Thompson next week." In a way I was glad he had a policy of not treating his own family because I felt he didn't trust me, and I sure didn't trust him. I thought he was just being nice because he had to. He was my father.

The next week Dr. Thompson said there could possibly still be strain, but he wasn't sure. He prescribed more weeks of bed rest. What did that mean? I wondered. What was I supposed to tell my friends about why I was always home now? But the prescribed bed rest was also comforting. If the doctor said I was supposed to stay home, then it must be right, and I could just relax. It wasn't a completely debilitative injury, but my parents seemed distracted by other family crises. They let it slide, and I gave in to the easier path. I was growing to like my quiet, private world when everyone was gone for the day.

A few days later Ann called to see if I wanted to go shopping with her and her mom. I longed to get out, but I couldn't walk very far and figured I shouldn't be going out shopping if I couldn't even go to school. The last few weeks I hadn't gone to ballet and really missed seeing Ann. We talked about all the juicy details of who was best friends with whom in ballet class, and she recounted the details of the football game the weekend before. Then she mentioned that Jacqui and Brenda, the "cool" girls, were coming shopping with her. "Don't you want to come?" she asked.

I shuddered at the image of those girls laughing when they saw me walking stiff legged in my splint. "I can't. Mom won't let me," I said simply, assuming Mother would want me to rest my leg.

Even though I was out of school, friends continued to call to see how I was, but by winter they stopped asking me to do things. I always said no. Our conversations grew shorter and less frequent as they continued on in junior high and I sank deeper into my inward-turned world. There was so little to talk about. I didn't want to complain about my knee, and there were only so many times I could recount the latest developments on the afternoon soaps. Strangely, the boredom took on a comfortable tone over the next months. The isolation I had initially balked at now felt safe.

The tension at home built by Christmas when Michael, too, began staying home from school a lot. He was tired and weak all the time, and at first the doctors said he had hepatitis. But in February they diagnosed his illness as leukemia and gave him little hope of living out the year. My knee ailment was lost in the swirl of fear and panic as the family focused on coping emotionally and physically with Michael's illness. Though he split his time between the couch across the room from me and a cancer research hospital where doctors were trying a new chemotherapy treatment on him, Michael was always with us. He was present in my parents' strained faces and in the increasing isolation we kids felt from them and each other.

By the time Michael was diagnosed, it had become normal for me to be home. Nobody really questioned it, not even me. It was easier to let me sit on the couch and be there as company for Michael. My tutor came three days a week to quiz me on English and math and give me homework, but otherwise I was left to myself. When Michael was home, we spent our days on separate couches, watching television or reading as we lay wrapped in sheets and quilts. When he was up to it, I'd bring in our favorite foods and we'd munch together. Later in the spring he was in a wheelchair whenever he wasn't on the couch and, like a little king, would direct me to get him what he wanted. Michael and I rarely ate together anymore because he was getting sicker. Instead, I'd grab a few cookies several times a day as I headed through the kitchen on some errand for Michael, and then stuff them behind the pillow on the couch to pick at without Mother seeing.

By May, as the other seventh graders were looking forward to a summer off, my entire world had changed. Although I rarely saw my friends anymore, Ann continued to call every couple of weeks. One warm Friday afternoon just before Memorial Day, I went to a yearbook-signing party at her house. She'd encouraged me to come, saying lots of our old friends from sixth grade would be there and she'd introduce me around to new friends. I felt shaky remembering the party in the fall, but I longed to feel part of the group again. I could walk a bit without the splint, so I left it home. I'd ordered a yearbook, and I had the slim white volume with the Harding emblem clutched tightly in my hands as Mother dropped me off at Ann's house. Getting out of the car, I tugged at my shapeless skirt in a mortified attempt to hide the forty pounds I had gained over the past few months. At five feet, one inch, I weighed more than 160 pounds.

As I walked up to the porch I looked through the window. My heart sank as I saw Ann laughing with her new girlfriends. I didn't belong here, and I knew it. But some desperate part of me was determined to fit in. Music blared through the open door as I entered. "Hi," I said, walking up to Ann's group. Last year — when I would have been running around checking on the food and music in the proprietary way of a hostess —

seemed like a lifetime ago. I wanted that role again; the security of that position meant I never had to look like I didn't belong.

"Hi back," Ann said as she smiled and introduced me to the others. We exchanged yearbooks, and then I went on to seek out the kids I recognized.

John wanted to know where I'd been. "Well, I've got this knee problem and can't walk up the stairs at school," I explained, hurriedly adding that I had a tutor. But it didn't matter. Before I finished explaining, Jean Ann had landed laughing on his lap.

I left within an hour, slipping out the side door without saying good-bye to Ann. She was preoccupied with refilling the chip bowl and flirting with Len. I was so glad I had told Mother I would take the bus home. Otherwise, I would have had to call her and wait to be picked up. Wandering through the block to the secret hideaway where Ann and I used to dream together, I leaned against a tree and looked at the laughing faces in the yearbook. I was there, smiling slightly in my pep club sweater. The pep club picture had been taken in the first few weeks of school, so I was included. Then I read the half dozen autographs of friends, blushing at the awkwardness of their words. Few people knew me, so few had signed. Those who did had scribbled something general about having a good summer. What else could they say? Words about all the great fun we'd had at football games, or struggling through algebra together? I'd worked on algebra alone with my doughnuts, between episodes of "That Girl" and "The Guiding Light."

As I walked in the door of our house, Michael called to me. "Heidi, is that you? Bring me some water, okay?"

From his plaintive tone I knew he was having a bad day. "Sure," I answered as I headed for the kitchen. Water in hand, I picked up a soda and a bag of potato chips for myself and hid them under the pillow I was carrying as I came past Mother. She was on the phone, arranging for Michael to go into the hospital again. My heart sank. But in a flash, as though the feeling had never existed, I put on a casual smile and walked into the living room. "Michael, you won't believe all the old friends I saw at the party," I said as I grabbed a handful of chips and settled down to give a glowing — and mythical — account of the yearbook-signing party.

The air was tense the next morning as Mom and Dad gathered Michael's things for another trip to the hospital. Each time he went, no one was sure how long the stay would be. The other kids were all at school; it was just Michael and me at home as usual. I tried to stay out of the way, curled up on my couch, as they rushed about. Michael was on his couch, and we watched a game show together. He looked drawn, and his eyes had the glazed look I now knew meant he was in pain. Most of the time he was cracking some joke, but whenever he was headed to the hospital he grew very quiet.

We both tried to ignore the strained discussion coming from upstairs. Then Mom and Dad burst into the room, carrying Michael's bags full of clothes, books, and games. "Okay, buddy, let's go," Dad said jovially, in a voice so different from the worried tones we'd heard overhead. Michael smiled wryly at me, but the edges of his mouth trembled. I watched as they moved out the back door, across the patio to the car, past where Michael's bike lay. He'd tried to get on it the day before, but was too weak and had fallen.

As I turned from the flurry of activity outside to the sudden stillness of the house, my eyes were riveted on Michael's couch. The covers were tousled. They're probably still warm from Michael's body, I thought. I always hated the moments right after they had left. There was a space where the voices still hung in the air, a space weighted by my fear that Michael's voice wouldn't be heard again in the room. Mrs. Manis, the maid Mom had hired to help out while Michael was sick, would come in a couple of hours to clean the house and fix dinner, but until then I was alone.

I looked at the game show blaring on television, then out the window to where my parents still struggled to get Michael and his things into the car. Then my eyes fell on the breakfast dishes, which I could see through the kitchen doorway. I could do them, I thought as I rose to hobble to the sink. But my altruistic attitude soon vanished, and I headed for the pantry where I knew I would find graham crackers and peanut butter. Pulling out a new box, the jar of peanut butter, and a knife, I headed back to my couch. Slathering a cracker with the creamy topping, I ate it in a couple of bites. I pulled out the latest romance novel I was reading. The heroine was coy and pretty, willowy in a fragile way that drew the hero to protect her. In this scene they walked along a cliff and he described how he would rescue her, how he would take her away from all the pain she had endured. I didn't even hear the car pull out of the driveway as it took Michael away.

That summer, with Michael in the last stages of leukemia, my sister Joanne and I were packed off to a fat camp. Joanne and I were both almost sixty pounds overweight. The evening of July 8 we stood numbly at a phone booth on the college campus as Mother told us Michael was dead. Joanne wrote down the details of our flight home. I just stared at the hamburger joint across the street. When Joanne finished talking, that's where we headed.

We stuffed down french fries as fast as we could. After a few minutes she turned to me with a slight smile and asked, "Want some more catsup?"

"Sure," I answered, and she got up to get more little packets. She gently handed them to me as she sat back down, and I thought that it was the first time I had ever felt close to her. Neither of us mentioned Michael's death, but we understood.

She squeezed my hand; then we self-consciously turned back to the food.

A few days later at home we were surrounded by all the food brought by people attending Michael's funeral. The brief bit of closeness I had felt with Joanne had vanished. In fact, I was confused by how my entire family was acting. Why didn't anyone look sad? With the house full of guests, Mother was in her usual flutter of activity and talk. Joanne and Amanda pushed me out of the kitchen so they could organize the food. The younger kids played in the backyard, and Dad was nowhere to be found.

Just before the funeral Dad had sat us all down in the living room and reminded us that we needed to be strong. He held a high position in the lay clergy of our church, and over the course of the past few months many people from church had supported the family and grown to love Michael. They grieved, Dad said, and we had to be strong for them. God would be proud of us.

Looking now at the smiling masks on my family's faces as they talked to visiting mourners, I felt confused. What about us? I kept expecting that pretty soon our family would be alone and we could talk about Michael, but nobody was making any moves in that direction.

Everyone looks so normal, I thought. I wanted to hit somebody, to make them talk to me. Then I saw my favorite pecan pie and, adding it to my already full plate, went alone to my room.

By the fall when I would have entered eighth grade, I weighed 180 pounds and had been out of school for most of a year. I spent my days as I had when Michael was alive, on the couch watching television, doing homework, reading romance novels, and eating. Time seemed to stop over the next couple of years as I remained in an emotional coma, rarely venturing out of the house except to go to church or on an occasional outing with the family. The pounds mounted as I ate more and more.

Shell shocked from losing his precious son, Dad sleepwalked through his days, fulfilling career obligations and never pressing to find out what was wrong with my knee. Mother rushed around trying to keep a family of six children together. That November I had an operation to repair torn ligaments in my knee. The pain continued, and a different doctor operated the next spring. It was exploratory surgery to see if the pain was caused by an extra bit of bone pressing on a nerve in the knee. It wasn't.

The summer after what would have been my freshman year in high school, Dad finally took things in hand. He did injection therapy on my hip, where a spasm was referring pain into my knee. It was a procedure he performed often on patients, and he had sensed this might be the problem but hadn't wanted to push me and risk alienating me. Within a few weeks the pain subsided. Suddenly I was faced with re-entering life as a 250-pound fifteen-year-old who had barely interacted with her peers for three years. I would be starting my sophomore year when the school year began in a couple of months.

🐛 🐛 🐛 🐛 🐛

In the weeks before I returned to school I scrounged to find patterns to make clothes that looked like the ones in teen fashion magazines. There was nothing remotely stylish in my size in the stores, so I decided to sew my own clothes. I'd been faithfully reading magazines and had an idea of what I wanted to wear that would give me the confidence I sought. I bought the largest size pattern available, added newspaper strips to the side seams, and it was my size. I couldn't make anything too complicated, but at least sewing meant I never had to go into a men's department for clothes again, as I had the year before. I had decided there had to be something other than the polyester pants I'd had to wear, and if it meant sewing to stay out of those, then so be it.

Around this time I began to distance myself from other fat people. But my attempts were in vain when Joanne was around. Even though we were three years apart, we were often lumped together as the "fat Waldrop girls." I hated it. Joanne was slovenly. I was different.

One day, a few weeks before I was to start school, a woman at church asked me, "How is school going, Joanne?"

I smiled and said tightly, "I'm not Joanne, I'm Heidi." I was furious at being mistaken for her. That afternoon at home I watched Joanne lumber around and fall into the chair by the television, stuffing a burger into her mouth. I'm not like her, and never will be, I thought. It was important that I separate myself from other fat people. I worked hard to walk without lumbering, and later to have an exciting career, and generally made efforts in every area of my life to compensate for being fat.

I spent my sophomore year at a private high school in Oklahoma City gulping for air like I was drowning, and searching for someone to show me the right way to be. The only way I knew how to be came from the one-dimensional characters portrayed on television and in romance novels. I had vicariously lived their romantic lives for almost three years, and now I needed someone to show me how a fifteen-year-old lived. I needed to know what a teenage girl wore, said, laughed about; how she reacted to boys, friends, and teachers. During the years of junior high school when kids learn how it feels to live their adolescent lives and test their notions of living, I was watching television, reading, and pretending. As a result, life in high school was an acting lesson for me — I played what I thought was my part.

I was eager to jump into all that I had missed. I took speech class, representing the school in speech competitions, and joined the yearbook staff and the pep club. But mostly I watched how people interacted, staying on the fringes until I was sure my actions were right. I was afraid of saying the wrong thing, and I reveled in the moments when I was in a group of my peers, finding the sense of belonging I deeply craved.

That year passed and, miraculously, I picked up the lingo and actions that had belied my lack of experience as a real teen. It was a good thing I learned fast because the summer after my sophomore year, when I had only a year of high school under my belt, my family moved to Grand Junction, Colorado.

I spent that June discovering English riding at a boarding camp. I had always ridden on a Western saddle, but now I entered a more refined world. Five other teenage girls and I learned about show jumping, and the precise and demanding art that went with the sleek, small English saddles. I loved it, riding several hours a day, mucking out the stable, and polishing saddles on long, warm afternoons. My father bought Sunny, a chestnut thoroughbred more suitable for jumping, but I still rode Dandy occasionally.

The fall of my junior year I dove into extracurricular activities with zeal, doing the minimum of school work required to maintain a B average. I participated in German club, junior music club, the yearbook staff, and choir. I was spared the embarrassment of gym class because of my knee, and I wheedled my way onto the seniors-only yearbook staff because I had been on staff at my other school.

But the best part was finally belonging to a group of friends again. Seven of us constituted the core of the group, but others joined us off and on to study, go to movies, or drive to the mountains for picnics. I had a crush on Tom, and when he called to ask if I wanted to go to the movies with the others,

I knew I was worthwhile. If a tall, cute, normal boy thought I was worth paying attention to, then I was okay, I deduced. I lived constantly with the uneasy feeling that people would find out that I wasn't the bubbly, fun-loving girl they knew. I feared that if my high school friends knew I had spent three years living on a couch they would think I was a freak. I worked hard to be outgoing and the best friend possible.

Other girls in the group were thinner than me, and I wanted to be thinner too. In my last two years of high school, I lost forty pounds. Part of the reason was that I went on Weight Watchers and stuck with it. The other part was that I was so happy with high school that food didn't seem important. By the time I graduated and headed to Europe for a six-week trip with a group of students, I weighed just over two hundred pounds, still heavy for my five-feet, seven-inch frame.

That fall I entered Brigham Young University in Provo, Utah. Classes were more difficult than they had been in high school, and everyone except me seemed focused on long-term goals. I grew restless. School seemed boring, although I did enjoy the excitement of new classes and loved football games and doing publicity for student government. But I was anxious to get out into the world. I continued through college in fits and starts, but never very enthusiastically.

Ever since I'd been to Europe the summer I turned eighteen, I had focused on the idea of going back for a longer time. Studying in Europe seemed the perfect solution to my wanderlust, so I joined BYU Semester Abroad in Salzburg, Austria. It was perfect: The six months of studies were easy to get through, and we spent weeks during that time traveling in the Middle East, Italy, France, England, and Spain. With forty girls — and no boys to create competition — I went on a binge fest across two continents. I had plenty of company; most of the other girls binged too. My weight ballooned back up to 260 pounds, but I didn't care. All rules seemed suspended in the fantasy world of Europe. But six months wasn't long enough for me. I stayed on to travel more and then lived with my sister Amanda, whose husband was stationed in the Army in Berlin.

But late that fall when I returned to Colorado to earn money for school, reality caught up with me. Even though I was only twenty, the damage I had been doing to my body began to show. I began having gallbladder attacks. The doctor said I needed to lose weight before he could remove my gallbladder, but two weeks later, I had another attack and was operated on anyway.

Several weeks after surgery, I began working in a local photography store and riding horses again, boarding my horse at the Whites' where I had gone to boarding camp. But that changed permanently one April afternoon. That Saturday I walked into the Whites' living room as I often did, yelling hello. Nancy returned the greeting and slipped out as Loren said he wanted to talk to me. He settled his compact, muscular body in a chair, and turned to me with his typically frank gaze. I tensed as I pulled out the chair across from him and sat down. Emotionally, I braced myself, although I didn't know why.

"Heidi," he began. "You know that when you ride on an English saddle all your weight rests just above the horse's kidneys. It isn't like a Western saddle where the weight of the rider is distributed over the horse's back." I nodded, feeling queasy.

"We've watched you ride, and it's damaging the horse with your weighing as much as you do. You need to lose weight or stop riding." It was as though he had punched me in the stomach or, worse, snatched my most treasured possession from me. The Whites were my trainers, and what they said was law. More importantly, I trusted their opinion, and it was painful to think of hurting my horse.

"I can't ride at all?" I asked weakly.

"I wouldn't recommend English, but we could put you on a big horse in a Western saddle," Loren said.

Cut out of the club, I thought numbly. "No thanks," I mumbled. "I better go now."

Loren tried to talk more. I had the impression he wanted me to take it as a challenge to lose weight; for an instant my anger flared, and I decided I was going to show them. Then I remembered that just days before I had gone off the Diet Center diet after being on it just two weeks. It was no use.

A sharp pain poked my heart every time I saw a horse after that. I'd counter it by telling myself that horses just weren't part of my life anymore. Over the next few years I'd come home and pet our horses like dogs. Then one time when I came home to visit I discovered that Dad had sold all four horses. I convinced myself it didn't matter.

When I headed back to college the next fall I began to really focus on my writing career. I had won a scholarship for a first-person article I wrote on my experiences in Israel, and began to believe I could make it as a writer. Writing had been my release for many years. I had felt compelled to chronicle my life from my days in grade school when brief entries in my locked diary told of my latest crush or slumber party. Later, I expressed myself in scribbled poetry and longer journal entries. Through high school my desire to write had grown, encouraged by my English and journalism teachers. But I didn't believe I had the talent to actually write. Instead, I thought I would go into a related field like public relations.

Winning the scholarship was enough encouragement for me to think about trying writing as a career. I took magazine courses and got a job on the student newspaper, writing free-lance articles for regional and airline in-flight magazines on the side. I loved writing for the cachet it brought me as the writer, and for the excitement and the sense of being a part of things that followed in its wake. Being editor of the school's weekly feature magazine was my entry to interviewing celebrities such as Kris Kristofferson and Harvey Korman when they came to tape "The Donnie and Marie Show" at the Osmond Studios in town.

One week during my second full year back at Brigham Young, I discovered how intrinsically the craft of writing drew me. In my magazine writing class, we'd been assigned to write a profile of a person. I had chosen a well-known local author. In the past, I had glided through interviews, relying on my natural curiosity, and then had dashed off an article by tying the quotes together in a readable fashion. This time it didn't work. Dr. Johnson, my professor, said he wanted some heart from it, and wanted me to consider who the man was and observe more deeply.

Furious at first, I went back and did more interviews with the author as well as his family, and pored over it during the next week. One day, even as I cursed my professor, I found myself caught in the delight of coming up with just the right word to describe the tilt of my subject's head.

My writing also provided the perfect excuse to escape the world and binge. I developed a precarious routine with food during college that would weave its fingers throughout the rest of my bingeing career. Living in a house with six roommates, I couldn't binge at home — nothing new to me, having grown up in a house full of siblings and an eagle-eyed mother. In high school, I had taken to eating fast food a lot, and now it became my mainstay.

Usually, the urge to binge would come on before I realized it. This particular night I had planned to stay home and watch television with my roommates, but when a commercial for Hostess pies appeared, I couldn't stop thinking about wanting a cherry pie. Within a half hour, the urge to binge was unstoppable. My job as an editor on the school newspaper was the perfect excuse for me to leave the house. "Listen, you know, I forgot I was going to cross-check the edit on a story that has to go into tomorrow's paper," I said as though it had just occurred to me. Jumping up to grab my coat before anyone could ask about the details, I mumbled I'd be back in an hour and shot out the door. As I got into the car, I hated myself for leading this double life, but I didn't know any other way to keep up appearances and binge too. I was sure my roommates would be appalled if they knew how I ate. Well, they were just never going to know.

Not wanting to be a total liar, I headed up to the newspaper room. I waved to Jim, the night copy editor. He was used to seeing me a couple of nights a week on these same errands of checking on a story.

My alibi in place, I headed to the grocery store. First, the pastry department, where I selected some cinnamon rolls and doughnut twists, then to the Hostess pies. Heading for the freeway, I drove north from Provo toward Salt Lake City, gobbling my sweets. About twenty miles later, I felt full and satisfied, but there were still some Hostess pies left. I turned the car around and headed home. I always bought the single or small packages because I knew I would have to finish them or risk putting them in my closet where a roommate might find them. This time I thought I might risk it, stuffing the remaining cakes in a brown paper bag and later sliding it in the back of the closet. I'd take them with me tomorrow when I went to visit Joanne, who lived forty-five minutes north in Salt Lake City. Joanne was the only person I would binge in front of. She didn't care, and I didn't care because she always ate more than I did.

In between my bingeing and my frantic social schedule, I worked hard on writing. I was getting published, and people seemed to like what I wrote. I got my first real magazine job that summer as an intern on *Friend* magazine, a religious magazine for children, published in Salt Lake. I took the internship rather lightly, interspersing my afternoons of research in the library with eating or napping in a rest room on another floor of the building.

The following year, after I had published many more articles, I tried out for the American Society of Magazine Editors (ASME) internship program, a program in which forty college students become interns at various national magazines. Only one person could compete from each school, and I was beat out by a more experienced student the first year I tried. But the next year I was chosen, and I spent the summer interning at *Family Circle* in New York. I felt like I had arrived one afternoon two months into the internship when I went to a cocktail party on the top of the Newsweek Building. Yet, even as I met editors I had idolized for years, all I wanted to do was hide under the table. I was sure they were judging me because I was fat, discounting any talent I may have had. I was never good enough, nothing I did was good enough — or could be good enough in my eyes — until I lost weight.

What do talent and hard work matter when you weigh 260 pounds? I thought as I stood on the fringe of the group, watching one of the other interns chat casually with a top editor. If only I hadn't gained so much weight when I was home with my knee, I moaned to myself. It all started with Thomas. Then Mimi's death and then Michael. My thoughts trailed away as I looked out across the skyscrapers of Manhattan. I knew I would never succeed until I had lost weight.

So, instead of going back to school that fall, I decided to go home to Colorado for a year and lose weight. I had a semester or so left of college, but with job possibilities already presenting themselves in New York, I figured I'd finish my degree some time in the future. I'd go home, lose one hundred pounds, and return to take New York by storm.

ঞ ঞ ঞ ঞ ঞ

A year later, I sat staring at the phone receiver I had just hung up, facing the prospect of going back to New York having lost only thirty pounds. I had just received a call from the editorial director of McGraw-Hill's magazine division offering me a job. At first I was ecstatic. As one of four editorial trainees, I would be on staff at five different magazines over the next year, and then be hired permanently at one of them.

This is a terrific way to start my New York magazine career, I thought as I looked out the window. Of course I had to say yes. The salary was higher than that offered to most other starting writers. There was no choice. Then I looked down at my body and a ripple of fear ran through me. I *was* looking better, having exercised some and having lost thirty pounds. My attitude was more positive and I felt better about myself. But I was still fat.

How could I go into that competitive world again as a fat person? Then again, how could I say no to McGraw-Hill? I couldn't. Besides, I thought, laughing to myself, you can't step out of life and solve your problems. Surely I would lose weight once I was in New York. Entering a new and exciting world would be just the thing to further encourage the development of my new attitude. I'd just keep the momentum going as I focused on the fun of New York. Images of Greenwich Village and the Statue of Liberty were already filling my head.

CHAPTER TWO

Living the "In Spite Of" Life

Fall 1980 — Summer 1983

I hadn't been at the party very long when I met him, and I was drawn to him like a magnet. Jonathan fit the look of what I wanted. With dark curly hair, an athletic build, and a chiseled jaw, he resembled the heroes in the romance novels I'd lived with for so long. Dressed impeccably in khaki pants and a simple white broadcloth shirt, he was leaning against the wall near the door when my friend Amy introduced us. "So, you're a journalist," he said, turning to me as Amy headed across the room to another friend she had just spotted.

It was the opening I'd hoped for because I could quickly equalize whatever first impression he had of me as a fat, though pretty and well-dressed, woman. "Yes, I got to New York just a few weeks ago," I responded. "I'm working at McGraw-Hill now.

"Today I was at my first big-time press conference; it was with the U.S. Secretary of Treasury at the Waldorf-Astoria," I continued, with just enough amazement in my voice to belie any hint of bragging. "It was incredible having to ask a question in front of all the television cameras! It was tough, but fun; you know, "NBC Nightly News" and all that," I said, laughing.

As I told Jonathan about my editor's instructions to ask a specific question if it wasn't covered by another reporter, I sounded only confident and excited. The memory was quite different. Actually, I'd been seized with horror as I stood in front of the cameras and audience of other reporters. I hoped against hope that the camera didn't show my entire body. Terrified of how I was perceived, I had tried to carry off a professional look by wearing a suit jacket over my size twenty-two flowered rayon dress.

As Jonathan and I moved across the room to sit, I was careful to walk beside him rather than in front of him so he wouldn't see the expanse of my backside. I tried hard to keep him occupied and focused on my face, asking him what he did for fun in the city. His latest passion, a game called bicycle polo, fascinated me. "Wait a second," I said, amused and skeptical. "I've heard of polo with horses, but bicycles?"

He explained that a bunch of his buddies had started playing the game, riding bicycles instead of horses, in a field in Central Park. "It's the same game, just with bikes," he said. "We've started the Manhattan Bicycle Polo Association and are going to compete with teams from other cities. It's a great urban game."

"That sounds like a load of fun," I responded. "You should try to get some publicity about the group so others will want to join," I continued, hoping he'd pick up on the idea and ask me to help. He did, inviting me to watch a game and attend an officers' meeting later that week. Here was the all-important opportunity I'd been searching for since I met him, a way I could see him again. As we walked out of the party, I felt like I'd accomplished some task, buying more time for him to see my sterling qualities behind the weight. It never occurred to me that he might simply want to get together because he enjoyed my company.

The next morning my girlfriend Wendy called to invite me to the beach. The beach! It was my rule never to go to the beach. Not only did it mean putting on a swimsuit, but actually going out in public in it. Automatic responses came to mind, excuses about other obligations for the day. But it would just be the two of us, and it was such a hot day. I couldn't actually wear only a bathing suit, but if I wore a sundress, well, maybe. What if she wanted me to go swimming? I could possibly hide my obesity from her by going in and coming out of the water after her, but what of all the other people on the beach? This monologue ran through my mind as I tried to listen to Wendy's enthusiastic plans for the day. I can't go around hiding all my life and letting this weight keep me from what I want to do, I thought defiantly. Besides, the only person who would see me that I actually knew would be Wendy.

After trudging out on the subway to Rockaway Beach in Brooklyn, and picking our way around hundreds of sun-bathers, we finally found a spot near the water. I sat down carefully and pulled off my sundress. I tried to appear casual as I draped it over my stomach and legs. I knew my upper body was big, but somehow it wasn't as repulsive as my stomach and legs. "Isn't this sun great?" I smiled with all the casualness I could muster.

"It sure is." Wendy answered as she pulled her shorts off to reveal a black maillot and her slim body. In the languid air off the ocean, we talked about life in Manhattan.

Wendy and I had been lying on the beach for a couple of hours when the Concorde, taking off from JFK airport, flew directly overhead. We sat up to watch its fluid silhouette glide into the horizon; then I shaded my eyes and surveyed the beach. My gaze slammed abruptly into the startling sight of three friends from church standing a short distance behind us. They were watching the Concorde too. Of all the beaches in New York, and of all the spots on this one, they had to pick this exact place, I thought. Cursing my own stupidity under my breath and grabbing a towel to cover my massive legs, I smiled and waved.

They came over and plopped down next to us. "What a fortunate coincidence," Sephora said as she sat down. Tony and Peter arranged their towels as though they were in for the duration.

No one seemed to notice as I tensely laid back down, arranging the towel to cover my legs and still look like I hadn't a care in the world. Suddenly I wondered if everyone around us was watching me. I imagined people's smirking sideways glances as they asked themselves how a woman so large had the gall to come to the beach. Unable to concentrate on the conversation going on around me, I finally gave in to the twisting inside me. After a half hour, I mumbled something about needing to get out of the sun, and Wendy and I left.

That night I sat down to write my parents my usual glowing account of my exploits but couldn't muster any enthusiasm. I felt deflated. Today's embarrassment loomed so large that the sparkling New York lifestyle I'd been so impressed with the night before felt like a sham. All those people at the party where you met Jonathan were probably laughing at you, too, I thought. What made you think you could ever fit in? Jonathan was just being nice. Suddenly I saw our interaction in an entirely different light, imagining that he had merely tolerated me, writing me off as a "sweet fat girl" rather than a woman he could actually be interested in. I blushed at how stupid I'd been to think he might have been interested in me as anything other than a friend.

When my roommate, Katherine, came in a few minutes later she announced that she would be joining me and a group of friends for a picnic after church the next day. My mind quickly calculated that that would mean she would be gone from the apartment all afternoon and evening. I couldn't let that opportunity pass by. "Oh, you know, I've been thinking that I may not go," I said, as though I had been considering it all day instead of only at that instant. "My sunburn is hurting, and I want to get some letters written. I'm not sure if I'll go, but I'll decide in the morning," I told her. But I had already decided, recalling the comfort of those rare afternoons in college when everyone was gone and I could eat anything I wanted.

The next day, I fixed a large lunch to the strains of Mozart, relaxed and content in my solitude. Afterward, I headed to the couch to write letters, but ended up napping. Waking about 4:00 P.M., I headed to the kitchen to do the dishes. I'll have to finish off the pie or throw it away, I thought as I cleaned up. It was half gone and Katherine would wonder why. If she never saw it, she wouldn't know it had ever been in the house. I put away the leftovers of the meal and carefully stowed the candy and chips in a paper bag at the back of my closet. The dip would have to be thrown away because Katherine would wonder where it came from.

I finished the cleaning, turned on the television, and settled on the couch. It was then I realized what I had forgotten. I really wanted those chocolate layer cookies. Katherine was due home in the next hour or so, but I couldn't be sure. She might come home early. Should I chance it? I hoped the store was open. It was only two blocks away. I grabbed my sandals and dressed quickly, practically running through the lobby and out the front door of the apartment building. That store better be open, I said to myself as I walked fast, my breath coming hard. Luckily, it was. Back in the apartment building, I panicked as I got on the elevator. What if Katherine was already home and I didn't get to eat any cookies? Before making it back to the apartment I had ripped the bag open and stuffed two down.

When I walked in the door, I casually called her name. Good, she isn't here, I thought. Dropping my purse, I headed to the couch and turned on the television, the bag of cookies nestled in my lap. Less than ten minutes later I heard the key in the lock and in one practiced motion slid the package into my oversized purse next to the couch, chewing as fast as I could and wiping crumbs off my mouth.

"Hi," I said, "how was the picnic?" She started rattling on, and my heart calmed as I realized she hadn't noticed anything.

"Oh, it was okay," I said of my day. "I did some reading, and it was good to have time to meditate," I lied. In seven hours all I had done was sleep and eat.

❧ ❧ ❧ ❧ ❧

One Saturday morning toward the end of September 1980, I received a phone call that transformed my first autumn in New York. It was from Tom. He wanted to come and visit, to see if we might have a romantic future. His words sent my head and heart spinning as they had so many times before. I'd fallen in love with lanky, dark-haired Tom in the first few minutes I had met him as a junior in high school. He was my image of a hero: part of a large, wealthy family, he had a low-key confidence that made him the natural leader of our high school group and that drew me to him at once. But being overweight, I never thought he would be interested in me. He occasionally dated in high school but never me. Yet often, when the group was out together, Tom and I would end up deep in conversation in a corner.

Over the next several years we became tight friends, going to the same college and staying in contact as we went our separate ways those four years. Periodically we would draw close for a while and would talk about how we should explore romance since we seemed to fit so well together. My heart would leap for a couple of weeks, and then hope would fade as Tom realized he felt only friendship. Even though this battered my self-esteem, I kept holding onto the dream that someday romance would enter the picture.

This cycle had seemed never ending until a couple of months earlier, when I was preparing to come to New York. Something inside of me released Tom and the hope of a future with him. I had a new, exciting dream to focus on: a great job and a bright future. At 230 pounds, I had a long way to go to reach my weight loss goal, but I'd lost thirty pounds and felt that something had changed inside me. Having begun to feel good about myself without reference to my relationship with Tom, I saw clearly that I couldn't pin my self-esteem on any man's opinion of me. For the first time I felt I could truly put my hope of a future with Tom behind me and reach for what I wanted as an individual. I sensed that New York would have a dramatic impact on my life, and I was excited to get on with it.

My new attitude turned some key inside Tom, and he began asking me out for the first time since we'd known each other. My emotions were split — part of me was gratified to finally be pursued, but another part was furious that he had finally come around when my interest was waning.

Our feelings for each other came to a head a few nights before I was to leave for New York. We began talking after he drove me home from a dinner and dancing celebration for my birthday in late July. We talked about how exciting my life was, and he commented on how good I looked having lost weight. "I've felt really close to you all these years," he said as we settled on the couch. "I've felt like we might have a romantic future at times, but your weight was always an obstacle," he continued, glancing sideways to see how I was taking his words. "Sometimes I felt like it didn't bother me, and I'd feel like we could marry. Then I'd realize that I couldn't."

Confident that my positive attitude and weight loss would be permanent, and feeling better about the image I presented now, I felt distanced enough to talk about my weight. "I've sensed that," I said, feeling a little superior and angry that he'd denied his romantic feelings for me because I was overweight. "I'm just sorry you've begun to feel this way when I'm ready to move on, when I don't know how I feel anymore."

We talked for a couple of hours about the past, and then Tom asked about the future. "You used to think about future possibilities. Do you now?"

Leaning back on the couch, I thought a moment before I answered. It felt so good to have the upper hand. "I won't rule anything out, but I don't feel the intense love I used to. I'm excited to go to New York," I said. We agreed to keep in touch, but when we parted, I felt for the first time in our relationship that my heart was free.

Now, a few weeks into my New York adventure, Tom was turning my entire world upside down, uttering the first concrete words to indicate I might capture my dream of living happily ever after with him. "I'd like to come out for a long visit over Thanksgiving so we can see how we feel about each other, see if there is a future for us," he said. He sounded more serious and devoted than I had ever heard him. I couldn't believe I was hearing the words I had longed to hear for eight years.

My elation quickly turned to fear. I suddenly felt cornered. I was sure Tom was remembering that summer, and expected that I had continued well with my weight loss. Unspoken, but implicit in his words, was the assumption that I would have lost even more weight by now to become the slender woman he wanted to be with. What he didn't know was that I still weighed 230 pounds. I hadn't lost an ounce in the two months since I'd seen him. Could I trust him to see past my weight this time?

My heart can't stand another round with Tom, I realized with a start. But of course I would give us both the chance to see if we had a future together.

Thanksgiving was too soon for him to visit. I panicked, immediately thinking I wanted every moment I could to lose more weight. My heart jumped as we talked, both out of hope and out of terror that a relationship with him wouldn't happen unless I was more ready — physically and emotionally. I felt I had so much to work out inside myself first. I wanted to tell him that it was too soon and that I couldn't handle it. Instead, I said, "Thanksgiving is bad for me; how about the week after Christmas?" That was about as assertive as I could be. I didn't think I could put him off longer than that; he was in such a hurry to find out what was between us. Still, Christmas would give me almost a month longer to lose weight. He agreed to come out after spending time with his family at Christmas; then we chatted on about other things.

I felt shell shocked as I hung up — the thought of Tom's visit demanded that I take some action. "This is my chance," I said out loud to the empty room. It's what I've wanted for the eight years of our friendship, I thought, as I grabbed a calendar and quickly calculated the number of pounds I could lose in the weeks before he would arrive. Three months. I could lose forty pounds if I worked really hard. As much as I wanted to see him and finally attain that ever-elusive couple status, part of me resented his intrusion into my New York lifestyle and the confidence I was building on my own.

I joined Weight Watchers the next day, but within a week had slipped back into my old eating habits. Caught up in the excitement of outings with friends, and keeping pace with the demands of my career, I let two months pass without dieting. Then, one day in mid-November, reality hit me smack in the face. I only have a month left, I realized as I lay in a mound of autumn leaves in Central Park.

Why couldn't you, for once, stick to a diet? I thought, both angry and puzzled at myself. Even when it may determine the most important thing in your life, you can't do it!

As I sat up, my anger suddenly changed direction. So what if I haven't lost any weight? If it's ever going to work for us, Tom will have to love me just as I am, I thought defiantly. Then I groaned. Will he ever be able to get past the weight to see how perfect we are together? But how could I expect him to see me as desirable when I didn't? I tried hard to picture myself as the romantic heroine. The image wouldn't come. It didn't fit with my body. I had to lose weight. Four weeks, I quickly calculated. Ten pounds, at most. It wouldn't even show on my 230-pound frame.

Within a week I was caught up in the magic that overtakes New York City during the holiday season, and I forgot about my weight once again. How fun it will be to show Tom the city when he visits, I thought. I ignored the other image on the edge of my mind, the image of his disappointment when he saw I hadn't lost weight.

My head felt clear about Tom as I went to take the subway to the airport to meet his flight the last week of December. Defeated about not losing any weight, I decided I would simply let the chips fall where they may. And, with Tom suddenly so interested, I finally began to question what I really wanted. As I waited for the subway I talked to myself about the situation. I'm not even sure I want this relationship, I thought, feeling confused about how to combine a romantic relationship with my own identity and career. For me, it's either a complete focus on one or the other, I thought, realizing how I had gone back and forth, almost daily, between wanting the Cinderella image with Tom and the glamour of New York. Did I focus on my career as a defense against getting hurt, or did my reservations about a relationship have merit? I was confused. I honestly didn't know. My heart said I wanted this man, but would he want me? I'd prayed to have God help Tom see past my weight, and I tried to convince myself that if we were meant to be together things would work out.

Seconds later all this rational thought was shattered when I brushed past an obese woman. She was messy, dressed in polyester pants and a shapeless dark coat. I felt superior as I checked my makeup. Now she sat right across from me on the subway. I couldn't avoid facing the reality that, like her, I couldn't cross my legs because they were too large. Averting my eyes and staring into the darkness of the tunnel outside the window, I tried to still the uncontrollable trembling rising from deep inside. No, I'm not like her, I thought, suddenly terrified. My brain seemed numb and unable to focus on any idea or scene that would give me comfort.

Tom and I rang in 1981 watching fireworks together in Central Park. Part of me reveled in the romantic setting and the fun of his being there, but I couldn't help feeling uneasy wondering what he was thinking since I hadn't lost weight. On New Year's Day we drove up to Stockbridge, a picturesque town in the Berkshire Hills of western Massachusetts, to spend a few quiet days. One night as we finished a late dinner by candlelight in a restaurant, I thought how beautiful and romantic the scene was, how happy I was to be with the man who meant the most to me. As we got up to leave, he patted my back like a pal and some painful chord from the past struck deep inside me. Just friends, my heart said. How often over the years had some chance comment or action reminded me that his feelings didn't go beyond friendship.

"Let's go for a walk before we head up to our room," Tom said as we left the restaurant. Strolling along the quaint streets, I was silent, my protective shell in place.

After several attempts at conversation, Tom finally confronted me as we came into our room. "What's wrong, Heidi?" he asked.

Suddenly, remembering years past and his switch in attitude over the summer, anger welled up in me. For once, I spoke just what was on my mind. "I don't know why you won't give this a chance. Why won't you show me the feelings you said you had for me?" I asked, suddenly sure I wanted a relationship with him. In some angry corner of my heart, I was determined to have it, no matter what.

"But you can't force the feelings to come on cue, Heidi," he responded defensively.

I felt like I had been slapped, feeling somehow inferior because I felt at that moment that I could never be the focus of romantic interest for Tom. I had an intense desire to run from the room, away from his words and from the truth he might utter about me at any moment that would smash my hopes forever.

"I sense you don't really want to make a decision now about us, but I do," he continued. I panicked. What did he really mean when he said he needed to make a decision? That he had really already made it and that I had lost? If we made a decision now, I was sure it would be to remain friends. I was stalling for time. I knew he couldn't accept my weight as it was, but if I held out the hope to him that I would change, then maybe there was a chance. There was genuinely so much I was learning about myself and I knew that sometime soon I *would* lose weight; I just needed time. This week isn't a fair trial, I wanted to say, because I'm still overweight. Heidi, this isn't about pleasing him, I thought, grappling for the proper perspective. It's about my growing and changing only for myself. It's about me being whole before I enter a relationship.

A sense of futility washed over me then, a deep recognition that I was powerless over how he would or wouldn't react. Looking out the window, I noticed the sky was brightening with morning. We'd been talking for hours. In a roundabout way, he'd been telling me he couldn't wait forever for me to lose weight and "be ready." I didn't blame him. What hurt so deeply was that maybe I had already blown my chance. I couldn't force him to love me, to touch me, to want me as his wife.

"I'm going out for a minute," I muttered as we ended our conversation and decided to get a few hours sleep before exploring the area. Pulling on my robe and slippers, I barely made it to the snowy balcony at the end of the hall before I began crying. Tom had hardly touched me since he arrived, let alone kissed me in a romantic way. At that moment I couldn't even contemplate a future. All I could think was that I wasn't touchable or lovable, and it tormented me.

"Why did I think it would be any different this time?" I asked myself. Pulling my robe more tightly against the very early morning air, I suddenly realized I had no idea whether or not I was actually attracted to Tom. For all these years, getting him to love me had been like conquering Mount Everest or something.

The chill of the air drove me back into the inn. I sat down on an overstuffed love seat. You always think if you act just right or say the right thing it will work out. Only all your orchestrations backfired on you this time, Heidi, I told myself. Would I never feel myself to be cherished and the object of romance? I looked down to where my body took up more than half the couch. Not while I looked like this.

By the time we were back in New York, my head and heart had settled back into a comfortable zone; for us, this was a "best friends" situation, with me always wanting more. At least it was familiar. I knew how to act, and more importantly, how to feel. Because we still hadn't made a firm decision, I continued to hope.

On the day he left, I slipped out of the office without telling my editor, and we headed to the airport. It wasn't until we stood holding hands waiting for his flight to be called that I wondered when we would talk to or see each other again. After kissing me lightly, Tom simply said, "Talk to you soon," and was gone.

The following Friday I came home for lunch to find an envelope with Tom's handwriting on it. I dropped everything and went into the bedroom to read the letter inside. The sting of his words was sharp. I read and cried, feeling like I had been physically struck when he said he was sure I'd be surprised that he'd come to a decision so soon. I wasn't. I had sensed it all along. He went on to say that it was obvious there wasn't any physical attraction between us. I felt cold and numb. He meant that he wasn't attracted to me. Then the letter switched tone to express how much I'd always meant to him. The pity was too much. I felt humiliated.

I could hear Katherine in the other room and knew I could never tell her. The idea that I had been rejected and that Tom didn't want me was so unspeakable that I had to get away from everyone to even begin to deal with it. I had to be free to feel this and weep freely. I took the train to a friend's empty apartment in Scarsdale, a half hour away, and went for a walk in the snow.

How many years had Tom messed with my heart by saying he only wanted friendship, but sometimes acting as if he wanted more? Then, when I had finally gotten rid of my love for him, he called about visiting me in New York. Well, at least this time I know that it's final, I thought. If not for him, then for me. Suddenly, as I looked at the clean white field of snow,

I knew what I needed to do. In the pristine smoothness, I sketched his name and then stomped through it, symbolically obliterating him the way I felt he had obliterated the hope I had held on to for all those years. When I returned to my friend's apartment, I was shaking and spent.

Waking on Saturday, I decided I'd allow myself the weekend to regroup, and then get on with my life as a writer in the Big Apple. Much as it hurt, I realized Tom had been right: Although the relationship seemed right logically, the appropriate feelings simply weren't there. Not for Tom, and not for me either, really. I had focused so rigidly on keeping him from rejecting me that I had been unable to ask myself if Tom was truly what I wanted.

Then, other questions came flooding in. Was it just the weight that had kept us apart? I wondered. Or was it that he didn't want to get tied up with someone who, being so fat, obviously must have a lot of problems? I couldn't ask myself these questions because I was afraid of the answers. The one thing left running through my mind was, Mother was right; no man will ever love me while I'm fat.

ॐ ॐ ॐ ॐ ॐ

I returned to New York with renewed vigor, ready to forget Tom and conquer the career world. As I walked home from work one sunny afternoon a few weeks later, my mood brightened. Heh, you're in New York, I thought with a start as I looked up at the glittering marquees of the Broadway theaters. Take advantage of it. You've got a chance as a McGraw-Hill editorial trainee that most beginning writers would kill for; don't let it pass you by.

Yet, as gratified as I was with the work I was doing at McGraw-Hill, it wasn't quite right. Most of McGraw-Hill's magazines were aimed at people in specific industries. These magazines were anything but household names. I wanted Mom and Dad to be able to go to any newsstand and pick up a copy of an article I had written.

I want to be published in the big-name magazines, I thought. I knew this was ambitious, but I worked for the right organization: I could start with *BusinessWeek*, McGraw-Hill's prestigious flagship. I'd already put my bid in for a rotation on staff there.

Through the spring I moved toward my goal in fits and starts: I would push hard at work for a couple of weeks, but then something would click off inside me. I noticed one day in late April that something was terribly wrong. It was mid-morning on a Thursday, and rather than sitting at my desk, I was sitting on a bench in Central Park — again. What am I doing here? I asked myself. Even though I had a stack of unfinished assignments on my desk, I had called in sick that morning. I *am* sick, I realized with a laugh: emotionally sick.

I'd awoke that morning and knew I couldn't face work. What scared me was that this kept happening every few weeks. What scared me more was that a couple of times in the past week I had told my editor I had to go do research at the library — and I truly intended to — only I'd end up at home eating cookies and then sleeping all afternoon. I had so much freedom on my job; nobody really noticed what I did as long as I completed my work. Even so, this isn't normal behavior, I thought. The pressure builds up inside me and I have to escape. Maybe it's the city, I reasoned as I got up from the bench and headed home. But I knew it was more than the stress of living in New York. As much as I focused on my career, I wanted so much to lose weight.

I didn't have anyone to talk to, either. "Where have all my friends gone?" I asked myself as I walked into my quiet apartment and sat on the sofa. Confusing images raced through my mind, the insecurities of a Heidi I didn't know. The week before, I had been afraid of introducing my friend Karen to Kent, another friend, because I thought he might like her better and I would be shut out. I also recalled that recently when I'd felt an intense need to talk to someone, I'd called several friends, only to end up making superficial chat about my latest press conference, without ever getting to the heart of things. What is it inside that just can't reach out? I wondered. I thought of all the people that I did things with, and there was no one I felt comfortable talking to about these strange feelings. Katherine would try and fix it. Alec would laugh it off, saying, "Get over it." And Kent? He'd just think I was crazy. Maybe I was crazy.

ぷ ぷ ぷ ぷ ぷ

In June, I joined the *BusinessWeek* staff, reporting and writing as an editorial trainee. From the first day, *BusinessWeek* both terrified and enthralled me. "Hi, I'm Heidi," I said tentatively as I walked into the cluttered office of the technology section editor, in whose department I would be working.

Lee motioned me to the chair and handed me a press release describing Polaroid's new camera. "I want you to cover this press conference," he said. "Review the information, then get down to the World Trade Center and see if it's worth writing about." Within a few hours, I was wearing a tag that read "Heidi Waldrop, *BusinessWeek*" and testing the new camera by photographing brightly colored balloons, clowns, and transplanted gardens.

It wasn't long before I began to feel like part of the crew, joking and talking with other writers and editors. But most entertaining were the FOB (front of the book) meetings every Thursday morning. More than half of the staff of 125 crowded into the conference room to discuss cover story ideas for the following week's issue of the magazine. The electricity in the room energized me, as story ideas about IBM and Exxon were tossed around as potential feature articles. The decisions to report a story positively or negatively could not only affect public opinion and stock prices but United States political policy and world events too. My excitement at being a part of this picture heightened as I watched some of the best and brightest journalists in the country defend their article ideas or come up with innovative approaches. I simply watched and listened.

After six weeks of doing mostly research and fact checking, with some reporting, I finally got my chance to write a story on new VCR technology. Could I come through? Did I have the right stuff inside, the brainpower, the savvy, the instinct, the vocabulary? As the writer, I would be receiving pages of raw reporting from *BusinessWeek's* bureaus around the world and would have to pull it all together into a cohesive unit. Luckily, under the group journalism operation, several editors would review my work before it was printed, so any problems would be caught. Even so, I needed to prove myself with this story if I ever hoped to be hired in a full-time staff position. I assumed that's what I wanted.

Two weeks later, as my deadline approached, I was chained to the typewriter in my office, with pages of quotes and statistics from reporters taped up on all four walls around me. I panicked looking at the many sections I had highlighted. Wondering where to begin, I sunk my teeth deeply into a thick cream cheese-slathered bagel. Okay, I'm ready, I thought. But first, a few minutes to relax with breakfast. As I chewed I thought about the past two weeks. I'd been so excited about the story, but paralyzed with fear about it too. For the last two weeks I had begun each day by doing research in the library, but within an hour I would give up and go home to sleep all afternoon. Psyching myself up the next morning, I would make a few calls for background information and head to the library again only to end up at home to eat. By the time this week had rolled around, the down time I was spending eating or sleeping was taking up most of my days. I was truly panicked. But the last two days have been okay, I thought. I've started getting some of the ideas together.

Now, turning to the typewriter, I tentatively began typing an outline of the points I would make in the article. In between thoughts, I slid my hand in the top drawer of my desk, which was just a few inches ajar, for a handful of M&Ms. As the bell rang for the coffee cart mid-morning, I grabbed my wallet and headed out the door.

"How is it going?" asked Julia, my supervising editor.

"Just fine," I answered confidently as we fell in step together. I couldn't tell her how lost I felt. I thought she'd wonder why I was chosen to work there. Picking up a doughnut and soda, I headed back to my office. With only one break, to duck out to the deli for provisions, I worked through until 10:00 p.m. The next several days were the same, only I brought my packages of cookies and pretzels with me, keeping them hidden in my desk and surreptitiously removing them when I needed them. Canceling plans for the weekend, I continued my sixteen-hour days through the next week.

As I took my best effort in to Julia's office on deadline day, I had no idea whether it would measure up. Would more time have helped? I doubted it. I knew I was out of my league and was regretting having tried to do it without asking for her help along the way. Part of me expected that I should have been able to turn in a perfect manuscript, and was sure they expected it. Now, that assumption seemed silly. As I handed her the manuscript, all I could think about was getting back to the office to the two brownies in my desk drawer.

"How do you feel about it?" she asked casually.

Edgy inside, I answered with what I was sure she expected: "Fine. Good." Then, covering myself to make sure she remembered I was a novice, I added, "But it's my first article, so I'll be anxious for your feedback so I can do better on the next one."

A few hours later, when Julia knocked on my closed door, I stuffed the remnants of a Twinkie in the drawer and asked her to come in. She had my manuscript in her hands, with notes and red-pencil marks all over it. "I'd like you to go back and do some reporting to fill in these holes. We've rescheduled it for publication in a couple of weeks so you can rework it," she said. I was crestfallen, and I guess she could tell. "Heh, it's natural to have some trouble on the first one," she added. "And come to me if you need help along the way, Heidi. Don't wait until the end."

As the pressure mounted at *BusinessWeek*, I realized the image and the reality of the big-time magazine writer were miles apart. I laughed to remember how blithely I'd signed on for this. It was great for my ego when, at a party, I could tell someone I wrote for *BusinessWeek*. But the high lasted only a couple of minutes, and then I would think about how I actually felt about work and get depressed. The pressure. The fear. Was this what I had come to New York for?

In recent months I had begun to withdraw from friends without even realizing it. It was partly because of all the work I had to do to survive at *BusinessWeek*, but there was a deeper shakiness that stemmed from that snowy day in January when I had received Tom's letter. I didn't seem to know how to behave with friends anymore. I felt embarrassed to call them and ask if they wanted to do something, always afraid they would say no. Or worse yet, say yes but not mean it.

All my life I had convinced myself that my weight didn't make any difference and that I was just like everyone else. But lately my weight seemed to be the only thing that mattered. Whenever I was around people I felt there must be a sign flashing overhead that read, "Fat and unworthy." I felt so out of place and uncomfortable that it was easier for me to be alone. Withering in my self-induced seclusion, I couldn't bring myself to put the mask of confidence and enthusiasm back on. I wasn't fooling anyone anyway, I reasoned. Occasionally I would get my spirit back, thinking that if I acted like a thin, "normal" person, people would somehow overlook my weight. I'd try it for an evening, or a day, but the reality of how I felt cut so deeply that I couldn't deny it any longer or pretend to myself that I felt another way. I looked at myself in disgust and was sure everyone else did too.

My efforts to get back on track were schizophrenic at best. I would sporadically try to return to the scenes of the past fall, when I had been full of life and hope. Sometimes it worked; most times it didn't. In July, the day before my birthday, I pulled myself together to meet Amy at the weekly bicycle polo match in Central Park. As the guys came off the field after the game, I noticed Jonathan coming out from behind a bush with a bunch of packages and a cake precariously balanced in his arms. Everyone gathered around me then and sang "Happy Birthday," endearingly off tune. Holding back the tears that seemed too close to the surface these days, and suppressing the urge to hug them all, I thanked them. Looking up from where I sat, I didn't see any of the blue blood or chic outfits as I had in the fall; I saw only the warmth in their eyes. As I walked back through Central Park that evening, I thought how ironic it all was: My first real surprise birthday party ever, and it comes when I feel least worthy of it. My friends' demonstration of caring seemed all the more precious.

As my time at *BusinessWeek* wound down, I realized some tough things. I'd been given my chance at the brass ring and failed. Nobody was asking me to stay past the assigned time, and I didn't want to. I saw it as failure because I knew inside I hadn't given my all. Some part of me had figured I could slip by and still get the glory, that I didn't have to pay dues. As the deadline had approached, I had worked hard on the VCR article, but I had wasted most of the time the first couple of weeks by ducking out to binge. Could I have done better if I had worked the entire time? I thought so.

In the fall, with about three months left in the trainee program and no job at McGraw-Hill that appealed to me, I began to interview for jobs at other magazine companies, but got no offers. I also began to write free-lance articles for other magazines. I came home one day in September to find a certified collection notice from a department store in the mailbox. Shaking inside, I opened the front door to find Katherine lying sick on the couch. I can't deal with anyone, I thought as I headed to the bedroom with a brief greeting. The stack of bills on my desk made my stomach turn. There were so many, and I never seemed to keep up, even with the low rent I paid sharing an apartment with Katherine. How would I ever make it? Without a prospect for a job, I suddenly wondered how I would live.

I could feel the pressure mounting. I pulled out my list of contacts and tried to figure out the next step in job hunting. I just don't want to play this game anymore, I thought as I tossed the pages down on my desk and flopped onto my bed. I mentally reviewed all the interviews I'd had with various magazines that fall and the contacts with editors I'd made through the ASME internship program. There were still some balls in the air, but nothing had come through. I turned back to McGraw-Hill. Could I stay at one of their magazines if I wanted to? I hadn't thought of it, so rigid had I been in wanting to work at

BusinessWeek or some other big name magazine. I longed for the McGraw-Hill job with *Electronics* magazine that I had so quickly turned down that summer because it wasn't just what I wanted. All my high hopes were fading as I faced the reality of paying bills without my McGraw-Hill salary.

Rolling over to bury my head in my arms, I wished my brain would work better, that I could understand what was going on inside. I was confused and consumed with self-doubt. I had no idea where my life was going or how to take control of it. Something is pressing me down and blocking my way, I thought, hugging my body tightly. Where has my vision gone? I used to have such a clear understanding of what I wanted. Why can't I find the strength to achieve my goals? I wondered. I felt so bound by not being able to lose weight, but it was deeper than that. I had a sense that I was ignoring some fundamental spiritual or emotional connection inside. I felt that I was cut off from God because God was mad that I wasn't losing weight. If I were a "good girl" I would be able to motivate myself and lose weight. It never occurred to me to ask God for help with something I considered so insignificant. But it isn't insignificant, a tiny voice inside me whispered. The thing that was blocking my way was more than the weight; somehow it was tied to the growth of my soul, but I couldn't see how.

I was emotionally bankrupt. I needed help. All my illusions of grandeur in the New York world had come tumbling down around me, so when a friend suggested that I see a psychologist, I put aside my long-standing prejudice that only "crazies" did that and jumped at the possibility of getting some answers. If only I could find out why I ate, I could control it, I thought.

During those first weeks with Patrick, my therapist, I was just interested in learning why I ate, and in talking about my depression and lack of focus on my career. Then one day late in September, I began to see my problem was much deeper.

I saw that something wasn't working right inside me, and I began to face the possibility that my ideas about life were distorted. As I got off the bus at East 28th Street and walked toward the tall building where his office was, I tried to put on my happy analytical face. But images of the night before, when I had reread Tom's letter between bits of chocolate pie, washed over me. I pushed these hurtful feelings down. Patrick and I hadn't discussed Tom yet, and I didn't really see the point. We were going to talk about why I ate.

A few minutes later I was sitting on his couch, fidgeting with the edge of a pillow and looking out the window. "What's been going on this week?" he asked.

"Oh, you know, the usual. It's really helped me to talk to you," I said, with a sense it was what he wanted to hear. But it wasn't.

"Heidi, what are you feeling?" he asked. A memory of the night before came, and with it a wave of depression. No. Not that. It was too close. My mind cast about for something to discuss. All kinds of things had gone on that week that we could analyze. Why did none of them come to mind now? Ah, here was something: my feeling of frustration over not getting a second interview at *Newsweek*. I smiled and told him about it.

Ten minutes later, he was pressing me again. "Heidi, what is all this lighthearted analyzing? What are you feeling? Now, right now?"

Okay, I could explain about Tom generally. "Well, there was this guy whom I've known for many years who came to visit last Christmas," I said as I sat up straight, speaking as though I were recounting the story of a cousin.

That worked until he asked what the letter from Tom had said and what I felt about it. The tears came unbidden as shame spread through me.

After a couple of minutes, I said, "I was furious, then I felt worthless, as though I were totally inept at relating to other human beings. As though I'll never fix what's broken inside of me. Never love somebody again."

As my tears subsided near the end of the session, I felt really stupid, and vaguely embarrassed that Patrick had seen me so sad and depressed. I was supposed to be perky and totally in control around other people. But, because we had developed an honest relationship, I felt able to express my embarrassment.

"Why do you feel embarrassed to show me your sadness?" he asked, puzzled.

"Because showing feelings like that is weak," I answered. As we talked, I remembered watching my father, who was so strong and who rarely showed emotion, and also watching Mother, whom I always discounted for her emotional displays. A key turned inside. I saw that I had been judging my feelings before I even allowed myself to feel them.

Somewhere deep inside I had always believed that showing angry or vulnerable feelings was not only weak but wrong. Feelings are not right or wrong, they just *are*, I realized. A feeling of great freedom opened in my heart then. I'm allowed to feel anything, I thought. I wanted to go out and try it on friends and see how they reacted when I just said how I felt at the time, instead of squelching my sadness or frustration because I was afraid they wouldn't want to be around me if I felt that way.

Over the next few weeks, I didn't feel the need to binge as much. And mostly, I found I didn't feel the need to hide my feelings. Food dulled my senses, and for the first time I didn't want to ignore those feelings. I wanted to feel them because I knew I wasn't alone with them. When confusion settled over me, as it often did, I was able to talk to Patrick about it. Now that I was free to express anything I wanted in that cocoon of understanding and unconditional acceptance that was Patrick's office, I looked forward to the sessions all week.

One day as I walked to the bus after a session, I was amazed at the difference in myself. Funny that the food and my feelings should have such a correlation so soon in therapy, I thought. I had no illusions that my life would change quickly, but I had hope. I could see the possibility of food taking on less importance to me, and it was exciting.

My thoughts continued as I got on the bus. I remembered my talk with Patrick that day about how I learned to stuff my feelings down and be who I thought I was supposed to be in the family so I would be loved. Afterward, I would eat alone in my bedroom. *Then* I had to, I thought as I looked out the bus window. *Now* I don't. I've been so frightened that I couldn't get off the self-destruct cycle. Now I'm beginning to understand why my life evolved as it did, why I hid out in food, and maybe I won't have to anymore. For the first time, I see that the burden can be lifted if I want to work on it.

But as I got off the bus, I realized that there were more immediate issues at hand. A job. Fear rose up. The idea of full-time free-lance writing had taken hold in my mind a couple of weeks before. I'll get control over my life by free-lancing, I told myself. I pictured a quiet little alcove with my typewriter and a box of cookies on the desk. All I had to do was meet deadlines. No explaining to anyone about my comings and goings. Once I began thinking about free-lancing, I couldn't imagine being locked into another staff position. Some fear came with that thought, though, the fear that if I took a staff position, I'd eventually be fired. I hadn't been coming through on the assignments at McGraw-Hill very well lately.

On the first of December 1981, I became a free-lance writer, continuing to live with Katherine at a low rent and turning our porch into a small office for myself. I reveled in the image, easing out of bed about 8:00 A.M. and having breakfast, then making phone calls, organizing files, and making lists until noontime when I would take a walk to enjoy New York at Christmas. By January, this frolicsome approach was slammed up against the reality that I needed to make money. Katherine had decided she wanted to live alone, so I was faced with the prospect of finding an apartment and paying at least twice what I paid living with her. I found a studio apartment through a friend who was getting married; it was on the east side of Manhattan — the rent was high.

The cold, cruel world hit me in the stomach, but there was still Dad to bail me out. Fear overwhelmed me the day I called to ask him for a loan. He had been strongly against my becoming a free-lancer. But he didn't say no when I asked for money. A few days later, I opened the envelope he sent to find a check for $550 and a note that simply said it was all he could scrape together and to spend it wisely. Opposing feelings hit me. Was I taking money he didn't have? I couldn't be sure. So often he had said such things just to impress the value of money on us children. Was he being a martyr? I asked in anger. Or is he really strapped? I wondered with guilt. Finally, a deep appreciation came over me for the money I desperately needed in order to pay the rent. But I didn't know how to express it to him, so I only mumbled thanks when I called to tell him it had arrived.

As I scrounged around for article assignments to pay rent those first months of 1982, I felt a world away from the Heidi I had been when I first arrived in New York. Sitting at my desk in my new apartment one morning in February, with only my new kitten, Sasha, to keep me company, loneliness spread through me. Just me in my solitary cocoon. It was what I had wanted. I could buy any foods I wanted and leave them out because there was no roommate to question what I ate. I could eat and watch television anytime, alone. Food, and the peace and quiet to enjoy it in. For the first few weeks that was all I did: eat and play at getting organized, pulling files together and calling editors to make appointments to show them my writing. I couldn't find the motivation, the heart, to begin to free-lance. I felt so overwhelmed by the task of finding work, and the bills just kept mounting.

৵ ৵ ৵ ৵ ৵

I sat at my desk for days now, hardly getting any work done. I felt numb and lethargic. The phone rang, and I jumped at it, desperate for human connection. It was Janna, a friend from college who now lived in New York too. "Hi, how are you?" she asked.

"Great, just great," I responded quickly. "I've got some good assignments and good possibilities for more." I pushed down the image of the overdue bills, blushing at the thought of telling her how bad things really were. She wouldn't want to be associated with a failure.

"You're such an adventurer. It's amazing that you're making it as a free-lance writer," she said.

Huh? I thought. I just had to quit before I got fired. But instead I responded, "It's tough, but I really want to do it." My bravado felt hollow. The image of being special as a potentially great writer was distant as I looked down at my messy desk and my fat, misshapen, neuter-looking body. I felt totally worthless and without talent. I used to feel okay about myself. Where had it gone?

Janna interrupted my thought by telling me about how Patty, another friend who had quit a magazine job a few months earlier to write free-lance, had just done a story on tennis player Martina Navratilova. My stomach clinched. I was missing the boat sitting here doing nothing. I had to get busy.

But I have to stay away from the old pressures that make me turn to food, one part of me thought again for the hundredth time. I have to get out there and earn money, another part said. My golden opportunity was growing dimmer by the moment. Where had all those cozy, softly lit scenes of freelancing gone? They had given way to the stark and painful reality of earning a living in a competitive field.

"Well, thanks for calling. I better get back to work," I said now to Janna, unable to contain the intensity of emotion that poured through me.

"We should get together sometime," she said.

"I'm so busy right now. Let me get through this deadline and I'll call you," I responded. The thought of actually being around her or other friends drained me because I knew it would be such an acting job on my part. I couldn't tell them the truth about myself and my life. I felt awkward every time I tried, my chattiness sounding so hollow next to the yawning chasm of pain inside me.

As I hung up, tears stung my eyes. What was I doing? I had let my polo friends slip away and wasn't interested in anything much these days. I longed for my early days in New York when I was able to keep up the bubbly, confident facade. Had that ever been a real part of me and had I just changed? Or was maintaining that facade so much work that I finally couldn't do it anymore? I wondered. This is the real Heidi: a worthless mess, I thought as I headed to the kitchen for a slice of the apple pie I'd bought last night. I'd spent my last pennies on it, going back and forth between it, a box of doughnuts, and a cake. I had only two dollars left until the day after tomorrow. I had two frozen dinners at home and enough salty, crunchy foods to last me awhile. The pie was what I needed.

Later that night, as I talked to Patrick, I still felt confused. "Why did I tell Janna I was so great when I felt so crummy?

I needed to talk to someone, but I couldn't let her know," I said as I looked at his dear, accepting face. "I was filled with confusion, but I couldn't tell her." He was still the only one I was completely open with. Much of the time I felt pushed and pulled by torrents of emotion, without feeling that I had anybody to hold on to, no one I trusted not to think I was crazy. I expected them, even Patrick, to grow impatient and weary with all my pain, to say I should have worked through it by now.

It was as though I were fighting some incredible battle against myself, one I sensed was life and death. I knew I had to change to be happy, yet I was so frightened of changing. And I didn't know how. I remembered, but still couldn't tell Patrick, about the Saturday night before. It was 2:30 A.M. and I couldn't sleep again for the fourth time that week. Having insomnia was so unlike me. I took out some sleeping pills, thinking I'd take one to get to sleep. I poured one out into my hand, then the rest. I counted fourteen, wondering whether that number would kill me. *Suicide.* The darkness and drama of the word seemed distant and unrelated to me; I just wanted to pull out of this misery. It frightened me to realize I even had thoughts of suicide. Good girls don't think that way — only sickies, I thought. You're supposed to be on the road to recovery with Patrick, I told myself as I poured the extra pills back into the bottle. A smooth, straight road, but it felt bumpy and jagged right then.

As I walked out of the session that night, I felt confused. Here I am learning all these new things about myself and my mistaken perceptions, but there isn't any list of rules to follow or moves to make to change myself, I thought. Some pieces of the puzzle had started to fit together, though. As I talked to Patrick about my conversation earlier with Janna, I realized that since I was a child I had been hiding who I truly was because I had always feared that my parents wouldn't love me when I was angry or depressed.

But now that I realize that, what do I do? Now surely I'll be able to lose weight or change whatever it is inside me that is making me so unhappy.

My weight and unhappiness seemed to be inexplicably linked, though I wasn't sure why. I felt like my weight somehow kept me from complete fulfillment and happiness. I was certain that taking risks, which I was afraid of taking now, would be easy when I was thin because I wouldn't be so concerned what people thought. I'd be normal then, part of the crowd.

By late spring, the "taking-care-of-business" Heidi had clicked into place. She had to. I racked my brain for ways to make money fast. I called editors I knew through ASME and came up with some ideas for articles that were accepted. I promised myself that by June 1, I'd be financially independent, and by June 3, I was getting there, with a combination of temporary secretarial work and some free-lance assignments. I didn't have to ask Dad for any more money.

As summer turned to fall, I began to work long hours, confined to my apartment writing and eating for days at a time, going out only to renew my food supply. I had been so focused on making money to survive, my goal of losing weight had faded. But as I came out of another emotional session with Patrick one day, I knew I had to get back to concentrating on weight loss. We hadn't talked about my weight. We never did. Instead, we talked about my family and childhood. But that night I stood nude in front of a full-length mirror, having decided that, with all this honesty, it was time to take stock of my body.

A further shock came when I joined Weight Watchers and found I weighed more than I ever had — 270 pounds. I suspected it, but wasn't prepared. Still, I didn't let it sway me from my course. It's a long way, I told myself, but I'll just keep at it. The first week, I went by the book, feeling refreshed and clean when I went to weigh in. I'd lost eight pounds. The next week I fiddled a bit with weighing and measuring my food and still lost five pounds. The third week began well, but then the games started: I began cheating here and there with extras or not weighing my food. I began saying I was "letting" myself have some sugary item or other, as if I were controlling it. But, in fact, it felt more like it was controlling me.

By the end of September the game was up. I went to weigh in and had lost nothing for two weeks in a row. Where was my initial discipline and enthusiasm? I was furious with myself, and I left before the Weight Watchers meeting even started. I really knew I'd lost the battle when, two hours later, I sat on my couch with an empty pie tin in front of me, having just consumed its entire contents.

Later that fall, I began working for *Electronic Learning* magazine, a magazine on high technology for teachers, as a temporary, full-time free-lancer. I was almost part of the staff, doing research, reporting, and writing either in their office or at home. I worked on other assignments and still did a lot of work as a temporary secretary. Working as a secretary or on *Electronic Learning,* I began to appreciate the discipline of a nine-to-five job. Most of the time I didn't freak out and run home as I had at McGraw-Hill. And I began to pay my monthly bills.

Still, finances were often rocky. Coming home from *Electronic Learning* one night, I found a notice in my mailbox: my landlord wanted two months rent or he would begin eviction proceedings. I was a month and a few days behind on the rent and had feared getting the notice for days. Why had I ever entered this risky free-lance world? I wondered as I plodded up the steps. My thoughts raced to calculate when my next checks would arrive. If I went across town and delivered the rent check by hand, it would give me two more days. But it still all depended on whether those checks arrived in the mail on time. The next morning I would have to call the accounting department at both magazines again to see whether the checks had already been mailed. As I pulled out my bills, I noticed three others that I had planned to pay when these checks arrived. I had arranged for the checks to come in the nick of time, and I prayed again to God that they would.

I felt totally deflated as I counted out the $16 in my purse and noticed there was only $55 left in my checking account. Enough to live on, but that was all. I felt guilty too because my bingeing cost a lot. I went for days at a time, even when I was low on cash, without cooking, living instead on expensive packaged food and items from the deli down the block. It really adds up, I thought as I put my wallet away. And I can't seem to say no to binge food. Eventually, the checks came, and I managed to squeak by one more time.

ϑ ϑ ϑ ϑ ϑ

With the spring of 1983 came a new energy. I was going to change. Some of my old heart had come back, the old competitive spirit and excitement at the opportunity New York offered. I began to write for new magazines with names my family recognized, and I continued to work for *Electronic Learning.* By attending more press luncheons and arranging to visit editors I met through ASME, I seemed to multiply my opportunities.

Though my career was taking off, I was in despair about my growing isolation. I felt like I'd lived for so long through others that I didn't know how to live my own life. I didn't think I had the skills. I found myself escaping more and more often into the lives of others through books, movies, and television — watching soap operas and feeling pain through them rather than coping with my own.

Insomnia, which had been only an occasional problem, became my nightly companion over the next several months. I would go to sleep at 11:00 P.M. and be wide awake at 1:00 A.M. A constant tense feeling plagued me. One night I awoke in intense anguish, fearing who I would be when I lost weight. The next night I woke planning to join Weight Watchers again. No, Diet Center. That would work — it was more controlled. I was obsessed on some deep level with finding the motivation to lose weight. What I need to do, I thought, is find the miracle key in my psyche that will explain why I eat. When I find that, it will unlock my prison forever. I felt cornered: All my excuses for eating were falling away, and the things I used to concentrate on instead of losing weight didn't hold my attention anymore. I was stuck, no longer able to delude myself and not ready to change. How long will I be mired in this inertia? I wondered in panic.

In August 1983, I got a call that pulled the rug out from under my illusions of how the world, and men in particular, saw me. It was from Troy, my high school pal who had had cystic fibrosis since I'd known him. He was in critical condition and was not expected to live through the night. He felt okay about dying and had taken care of everything except saying good-bye to me and another high school friend. I didn't know what to say, but then I realized all I needed to do was listen.

"I wanted to say I'm sorry," he said in a raspy whisper. I was confused. What did he have to be sorry about? Then he continued. "I was never kind enough to you because I had hang-ups about people who are overweight. I judged you and talked about you behind your back. If I live I won't ever again judge someone by their waistline," he said as he cried.

Anger and a sense of betrayal flared inside me, but now wasn't the time to express it, I reminded myself. He was sincere and needed to clear his conscience. As he talked on about the good times and expressed his appreciation for me, I had trouble concentrating. We talked about how he felt about dying, and he said he'd been bitter but now felt peaceful. Finally, he said that he loved me and said good-bye.

After I hung up, I sat in shocked silence. How could I have been so dense as to think Troy and I had had a good relationship? I asked myself. My mind jumped to all the other relationships where I had thought my weight didn't matter. If I had thought Troy wasn't judging me for my weight when he had been, what did it say about my understanding of what my other friends thought of me? His call jolted my very foundations and my perception of how others saw me. It brought up the self-hatred I thought I had begun to lay to rest. I sat for a long time despising myself for my weight; the raw knowledge that it did matter immobilized me.

It was with the need for sympathy and coddling that I went to my session with Patrick the next day, ready to recount the wrongs I had been done as a fat person. I was certain he would stand with me against Troy and an entire society that judged me as a fat person. Weeping, I talked about how it wasn't my fault that I was fat, again telling him about how my childhood and the years with my knee had scarred me. I then turned the talk to my anger at Troy, at men, and at society for judging me because of my weight. I told Patrick that I kept trying to find a man — Tom or any other man I was interested in — who would love the woman I was inside, in spite of my weight.

The real situation between me and men I was drawn to was quite different, however: My fat and defenses in place, I simultaneously demanded that the man love me and defied him to. When he didn't, I slid him into a place in my mind next to all the other shallow men, and assumed my role as a martyr with a heart of gold. Contempt oozed out of my every word as I spoke with Patrick.

Patrick simply looked at me and said, "Do you really believe that a man could be physically drawn to a woman twice the normal size?" I was stung, as though he'd slapped me. I felt he had betrayed me profoundly in posing this taboo question. I already knew the answer, but I couldn't bear it. Instead, I focused on the injustice of his words.

I sat numbly, nodding my head in apparent agreement as he talked on about facing the truth about what my weight meant in my life. This was just what I had always done with my father when I was too hurt to react to one of his lectures.

I'll give him the reaction he wants and keep up the wall, I thought. Then I'll go somewhere alone to feel.

I couldn't let Patrick see the raw pain I felt. Although his words had been anything but harsh, the truth behind them had caused pain, and now Patrick wasn't to be trusted. Didn't he know we weren't supposed to talk about my weight in this room? It was the safe place, the place where we talked about the history of the weight, the emotions behind the weight, but never about the weight itself — until that day.

CHAPTER THREE

Tiny Steps Out of the Cocoon

Winter 1984 — Summer 1984

As the lights of New York City faded behind me on Route 95, all I could think about was a Big Mac. But it was really a Big Mac *and* mounds of french fries I wanted. Now, I stood at a McDonald's beside the freeway just over the Connecticut border, appearing to contemplate the menu while my mind raced. How could I order all I wanted without the woman behind the counter thinking I was an obese glutton? I decided to follow my usual technique: Without a hitch in word or action, I approached the counter. "Let's see, what did Sharon and Victoria say they wanted? Hmm." Just the right amount of pause, then: "I'll have a small Diet Sprite and an order of french fries. For the others, a small Diet Coke, a chocolate milk shake, a Big Mac, and two orders of fries." I always ordered different drinks to throw them off.

I felt smug as I carried my cache back to the car, already tasting the special sauce in my mind. Sliding into my seat, I grabbed a handful of the spiky, greasy potatoes and simultaneously turned the ignition. After easing the car back onto the freeway, I polished off the rest of the food. As I sipped the last of the milk shake, my mind turned to something solid and sweet that would constitute a real dessert. Catching sight of a grocery store, I stopped to stock up on basics — Pepperidge

Farm cookies, Doritos, and Dr Pepper. Other stuff, like fresh fruit and canned goods, could wait until tomorrow, when I moved into my new home.

Already, I felt better knowing I had all the essentials on hand. I couldn't go very long without a fix. The tension in my stomach eased as I pulled a Mint Milano cookie out of the bag and sunk my teeth into it. I looked at my watch. Two hours out of the city. My stomach ballooned with its load, and the familiar numbing lethargy set in. My mind dulled, and I floated along with the music in my dark, safe cocoon speeding north.

About an hour later, a flicker of fear pushed at my sugar-fogged brain. Had I done the right thing, leaving my life in Manhattan for six months to move to Stonington, Connecticut? I stared into the darkness ahead with trepidation. On the surface, my reason for moving to the small fishing village on the coast seemed adventurous. An editor at a romance book publisher had seen some of my writing and suggested I try writing a novel to fit their genre. Since I had been a big romance novel reader as a teen, I was sure I could do it.

I hadn't really thought of moving until three months earlier, on a weekend in October, when the pieces suddenly seemed to fall together. A friend of mine, Sandra, and I had visited Stonington to see the leaves turning on New England's maples. We took Amtrak to Mystic, Connecticut, and took a taxi to the tiny peninsula community called Stonington five miles away. That day we explored the dozen or so blocks that make up the village.

On Sunday morning of that weekend, I wandered about the town. That was when I met Margaret Jansen, the owner of a little antique store on the main street. Minutes into our conversation in her overstuffed store on the first floor of a rambling house, she mentioned that a small studio apartment on the main floor that would become available in January. I quickly calculated how I could fulfill my dream to live in such an idyllic place. I would continue to write free-lance articles for magazines, but cut back the number I turned out so that I could write the romance novel. A friend was looking to store his car outside of the city, so I could take it. And I could sublet my Manhattan apartment to Sandra, who happened to be looking for a place to stay for a few months until she got married. The pieces had all fallen into place so smoothly.

I told everyone I was heading to Stonington to write my novel, and that with Stonington's lower cost of living, I would have more time to spend doing it. Part of me really believed that. But as I listed the pros and cons, I realized that this move was one more attempt to gain control over my life and my weight, which had finally hit the three hundred-pound mark. If I organized my life well enough, cut out the pressure of my fast-paced career, and refocused my priorities, I was sure that I could lose weight. I knew I'd have a better chance to reorder my daily habits in a more serene location.

I greeted the first morning in my paradise optimistically, unpacking and organizing as I munched on cookies. Just before noon, I noticed Margaret coming down the path at the side of the house, and my heart skipped a beat. My glance flickered to the kitchen table and the bags of cookies and candy stacked there. I grabbed them all in one practiced motion, sliding some into a box and stuffing others into the fridge. Then, I quickly changed my ratty sweatpants for jeans and ran a comb through my hair.

Just then came a knock at the door. I opened it with what I hoped was an innocent look on my face. "Welcome," she said with a smile and an inquisitive glance past me into the room. "I just wanted to stop by and see if you needed anything. Is the phone hooked up?"

"Yep, it's fine," I answered, turning slightly to close the door and discourage conversation.

"We'll introduce you around. It's an awfully small town," she continued in a mother-hen tone. A hint of a Southern accent in her voice and a tendency to pat my arm as she talked banished all images of the cool New Englanders I had counted on keeping at a friendly distance. My stomach tightened at the thought of being overrun by inquisitive and helpful neighbors.

"That's fine," I quickly said, annoyed at the proposed intrusion into my solitary world. I'd use the same excuse I had for years, I thought. My writing. "I'm up here to write that novel, you know. I'll be really focused on it. But I'd love to meet your friends sometime," I lied, in horror that I'd appear anything except friendly and gracious. I'd just be out a lot.

Later, I stood at the window angrily devouring a cookie as I watched Margaret's husband, Jack, putter around the back garden shed. I felt like a caged animal, listening to Margaret rustling around in the store and Jack walking past my windows along the side and back of the house as he worked. What if I wanted to be outside in my own backyard, wearing sweats and with my hair unwashed? Could she hear the television through the wall and know I was watching soap operas? Would they be stopping by all the time and see what I was eating? I grabbed another cookie.

Great, the dialogue with myself continued, I'll still have to hide what I eat. What would they think of me if they knew how sloppy my work and living habits really are? I'd been able to keep up the illusion of being the consummate New York professional because no one was really close enough to know about my down time. What would the Jansens think if they knew, and how could I keep them from finding out when they could pop in at any time? I realized, as I stood there, that some part of me had chosen to step out of New York so I didn't have to lead that double life — one where I worried what people knew about my habits and what they thought of me. I resented that it would probably be foisted on me again.

Okay, I can do this, I resolved. I just had to find out what the Jansens' habits were and not let myself fall apart when they were likely to be around. And there were shades on my windows. I'd keep them down. They couldn't guess that I wasn't working if they didn't hear the typewriter. Maybe they would think I was editing my writing when they didn't hear typing. And, I'd keep the television low. My mind was already weary from figuring out what they were thinking about me and how I could make them believe what I wanted them to, make them see the efficient, disciplined person I wanted desperately to be.

Looking down at the four cookies I had just grabbed, I remembered with a start why I was here. I had all that self-discovery to do and so much weight to lose. Putting the cookies back in the bag, I threw the package ceremoniously into the garbage and sat down at the kitchen table with paper and pen to set some goals. *First, exercise:* I would get the tires on my old bike fixed, and I would take a walk each day. *Next, food:* I would write down everything I ate and plan meals with fresh fruits and vegetables.

My eyes drifted to the edge of the cookie package in the garbage. No. No more snacking. No more sugar. I made out a menu for the night. Broiled chicken, fresh steamed broccoli, and an apple for dessert. A few minutes later, smiling sincerely at Jack, I walked out the back door to explore the town and find a grocery store. There's nothing to be afraid of, I thought. I don't have to hide anymore. I'm going to eat healthily, exercise, and work productively. Silly, all those feelings of being confined, caged; all the false gestures and dishonesty. That was the old Heidi.

Diagonally from my building was a deli. Unconsciously, I was drawn to its windows and found myself mentally taking stock of the various pastries in the case and the types of sandwiches on the menu. Shaking my head, as though to rid it of such thoughts, I headed to an innocuous magazine store across the way. Just two blocks away was my goal for this healthy food hunting trip: Roland's Market, a turn-of-the-century grocery store with worn wooden floors and an air of cozy mustiness. Bins just inside the door were piled high with fresh fruit, vegetables, and breads. Next to them was the snack aisle.

Without a glance, I passed the bags of potato chips and walked to the meat case, asking for a chicken to broil. As I perused the nearby shelves, a voice said, "You might want to try the low cal vegetable soup." I turned to find a man stacking cans, wondering why he was interested in what I ate. The expectant look in his eyes told me he was another talker with helpful advice. I was painfully familiar with what a small jump it was from advice on soup to "you have such a pretty face, you should lose weight." Smiling stiffly, I rapidly moved on to get the broccoli, the apples, and some crackers. The polite and questioning smile from the woman at the cash register reconfirmed my feeling that my shopping here would be limited. It's too personal, I thought, as I headed for the door.

A quick survey of the four-block downtown told me that this was the only grocery store in the village. Getting in the car, I drove into Mystic. With a sigh of relief I spotted a vast supermarket just inside town, and found plenty of Sara Lee goodies in the frozen food section. I stuffed all varieties in my shopping cart. Arriving home with my packages, I pulled down my shades, turned on some music, took out the brownies, and put the rest of the groceries away.

♨ ♨ ♨ ♨ ♨

A few days later, as I cleaned the refrigerator, I found the untouched chicken going bad in its wrapper. As I tossed it on top of a pizza carton and candy wrappers in the garbage can, I remembered my clear resolve my first day in Stonington. Where had my mind been? I stared numbly at the decaying food, feeling that I'd never be able to keep a commitment I made to myself or anyone else.

I felt as though I'd been waiting forever for that inner part of me to be *ready* — to want to lose the weight enough to sustain the work it involved. It wouldn't happen. How do I make it happen? I asked myself in frustration. The thought of my life continuing as it was terrified me. It always came back to the knowledge that there were no alternatives, only procrastination. I must lose the weight to be happy and productive, I thought as I gathered the garbage to throw it out. Yet I struggle so for the motivation to change and the guts to carry it through. The desire is so fleeting: I feel the heart of it at one moment, and the next all I want is to escape in sleep and food.

I was always going off to some place, stepping out of my pressured life as though I could stop the world and figure out where to go next. Only I never did. I simply denied reality for a few months and then stepped back on the treadmill. I'd come to Stonington hoping again to stop the cycle, although I wasn't quite sure what the cycle was. After I stuffed the garbage in the can outside the back door, I sat on the step and focused on understanding what it was I wanted to change. I knew I had to make a conscious choice of what I wanted instead of going along as I had, just doing enough to get by.

I'd been lucky . . . the summer internship at *Family Circle* magazine . . . writing on staff at *BusinessWeek*. It all sounds good for a few minutes at a cocktail party, I realized. But I've never really wanted anything except to lose weight and be one of those self-assured women I saw around me. Women who seem to like themselves.

I rode a roller coaster in my attempts to change my habits. Whether I was on track or not seemed out of my conscious control. There were weeks when things seemed to come together. I would attend Weight Watchers, work, and exercise on a schedule. But the next week I was back to bingeing, watching television, and sleeping, wishing the world would go away. My whole existence seemed to revolve around this internal struggle in my self-imposed isolation. I longed for someone to talk to, someone to bounce all these crazy ideas off and see what it was I was missing. But in Stonington I had carefully constructed a world of nothing more than acquaintances. So, instead of turning to friends, I turned to my journal. It had come to replace people for me over the weeks. When I ached, I wrote. Yet even writing didn't seem to help anymore. I was just talking to myself, and *I* didn't have the answers.

One night, after I had spent a typical day writing in my apartment, I was restless in my isolation. I decided I wanted to see a movie; movie watching was one of my frequent escapes. *Racing with the Moon* was showing at a theater nearby, so I went. In one scene of the movie, the two romantic leads embraced, the woman running her hand over the man's shoulder as they kissed. My heart wrenched, and a sudden longing to be held poured through me. In a split second it was gone, squashed so I wouldn't feel the profound pain.

But later, as I drove along the highway, something came back. Not even a thought or memory, only a reason to cry. Crying for myself, a woman so afraid to feel pain that her mind pushed it out before the feelings came in. I was more aware than ever before of the protective shield of fat that had surrounded me most of my life, at once a security and a prison. How easily

I pushed down the needs and wants of a normal human being. I ignored my need for other people, and I cried or felt only through soap operas.

My mind searched for something or someone whom I felt strongly about. Everyone — my family, old high school and college buddies, church and work friends — was dispensable. They had to be; otherwise I got hurt. I would emotionally toss them out the window at the slightest indication that they had betrayed my trust. Panic slapped me. Am I capable of love? I wondered. That question had run through most of my mental meanderings for months. The possibility of discovering the answer terrified me.

Later in the week, a girl from the church I was attending in Stonington called to invite me to a party. We chatted, and she seemed surprised to find I was living alone — as though I were so adventurous. Hanging up the phone, I laughed to myself. It's easier to head off somewhere new than it is to find the courage to stay and deal with relationships, I thought. Even as I'd said good-bye to friends and promised to call, I was relieved not to have to play the mind games of figuring out how to be a friend. Alone in Stonington, it wasn't necessary.

I remembered a few nights earlier when I had called Janna in Manhattan because I was feeling lonely. Throughout the entire conversation, I was afraid to tell her how miserable I was, sure she wouldn't want to be friends with a "loser." When I hung up the phone that night, I felt anxious. Nobody had given me a script for friendship, and I felt awkward whenever I needed a friend. Did I ask too much about her and seem to pry? Had I called too often or sounded too needy? I didn't know. I felt like I had as a teen, struggling to understand the rules. My head hurt from trying to decipher it all. For now, I thought, I'll just focus on spending time with myself and figuring out what's going on inside me that keeps me from losing weight.

♨ ♨ ♨ ♨ ♨

My safe little world in Stonington felt claustrophobic all of a sudden. I saw it as a world similar to the one I had created years ago on the couch, a world of nothing but work, food, television, movies, and books. My best friend, once again, was my journal. I was insulated from the expectations and demands of New York. My weight wasn't as out of place here, not the oddity it was in the goal-oriented world of the city. I didn't have to do anything except make money. What a simple and undemanding world I had designed. It wasn't to last long.

One morning in late April, I woke to the sound of shuffling and grunts. Both were coming from the center stairwell leading to the second floor apartment. After dressing, I went out to investigate and saw a jean-clad girl directing two guys with boxes up the stairs. *Pixie* was the word that came to mind as I looked at her cap of shiny brown hair and the slim, graceful petiteness that made me feel the size of an elephant. Immediately my defenses rose. I emotionally prepared for the judgment of my weight and superiority that I always expected from slender, attractive women. I was therefore taken aback by the gentle mirth and acceptance in her warm eyes as she introduced herself as Elizabeth, my new neighbor. She said she had just taken a job teaching children at the Mystic Aquarium, helping the kids learn about marine life by working directly with the live dolphins and sea lions on display at the museum.

Just then her roommate came bouncing through the door. All twinkling eyes and laughter, Emily was alive with the excitement of a child. "Have you seen that garden out back?" she asked Elizabeth. "It will be great for lazy, summer evenings — with tons of friends," she ended exuberantly. Then, before Elizabeth or I could speak a word, she turned and offered her hand to me. "Hi, I'm Emily," she said and launched into chatter about her job at Mystic Seaport, a re-created seventeenth-century whaling village, and about the recreational sailing she and Elizabeth did on weekends.

The big old house seemed to come alive after that, with Elizabeth and Emily coming and going all the time. One morning a week or so after the two moved in, Elizabeth and I sat in the back garden talking. We laughed about how our lives meshed in our shared quarters. "I can always tell who's home by the way you guys walk. Emily has such a heavy step," I said. "And, that third pair of steps I often hear is Emily's boyfriend, right?" Elizabeth began to giggle, shaking her head yes. "You'll be really confused later in the week when my boyfriend, Brian, comes to visit, because he hops around on one leg early in the morning before he puts on his wooden leg," she said, adding, "He lost his leg to cancer when he was twelve."

One day a few weeks later, we sat in her kitchen looking out at the misty grayness of the New England coast and eating turkey sandwiches. "You look like you've lost some weight," she said as we sat down.

Smoke and shadows, I thought. It's probably the combination of my new haircut and highlights. "Thanks," I said, and then felt compelled to go on. We hadn't talked about my weight yet, and I was sure it was on her mind. I better explain.

"I'm glad to finally be losing weight. I've been overweight since I was twelve when I was out of school and flat on my back for almost three years with knee problems. Mother said I would never be happy until I lost weight, and I guess I've held on to it all these years to prove her wrong. To prove I could make a life for myself in spite of the weight." I talked on, explaining the intricate psychology of why I was still overweight, hoping she wouldn't think I was just some fat slob.

A week or so later, I sat in my bed listening to the simple sounds of life above, growing more depressed by the minute.

Emily was gone for the weekend, and only Brian and Elizabeth were home. I heard bacon sizzling in a skillet, steps, laughter, and even the occasional sentence as Brian talked on the phone. All attempts at focusing on the book I was reading were thwarted by the relentless course of my mind. I imagined all the camaraderie and love that accompanied those simple sounds.

Earlier that afternoon, Brian had been off somewhere and Elizabeth was doing things around the house. I could hear the lightness in her step and remembered — with flashing clarity — the feeling and attitude you have toward the whole world when someone you love is expected soon. Now that Brian had come home, I could almost slide inside her and mimic her soft touch, hushed voice, and lilting laughter. Looking out the window, I tried to detach from the sounds. I was unintentionally part of the scene without Elizabeth and Brian even realizing it, yet I was so far from it in my solitary misery and longing that I might have been on another planet.

What would it feel like to have had a magical, carefree love in my early twenties? I didn't know; I had never had it. I looked down at my fat and despised it, resented it as if it were a person who had cheated me out of the love I heard upstairs. Then, instantly, I was angry at God for thrusting this on me. I could hear them speaking quietly to each other. A simple act, but I could barely stand the pain of wanting it. I wanted to run outside and away until Brian left. Each hushed tone sent an unmistakable message: You don't have it. You never will as long as you're fat. Moments later, the raging emotions were replaced by a deep sense of loss. Snatches of what a thin Heidi could have had in her twenties tortured me, and I felt as though someone had died.

An uncomfortable feeling of jealousy licked through me. I was jealous of Elizabeth's easily maintained, slender, agile, and unmarred body. I was jealous of her having someone to love and be loved by. But mostly, I envied the straightforward, self-assured way that Elizabeth dealt with life and how she felt at home in her skin. My mind searched for someone to blame, but there was only me. Yet I could be part of that world. Only I, myself, held it off. That's what made it harder. I knew I kept myself from it, but I couldn't figure out why. Somehow I believed that if I were thin I would challenge myself more and show up for life as my whole and true self, unafraid of others' opinions.

Monday morning, after Brian left, I groaned and rolled over in bed as I heard Elizabeth's light step on the stairs. As the front door closed, something drew me to the window to watch her dash across the street and hop into her car on her way to work. My body felt so heavy. My soul felt so heavy. I thought of how she was always coming and going, planning and doing, as I sat in my apartment only living about half the time. This isn't the way to live, I thought.

ॐ ॐ ॐ ॐ ॐ

The Friday evening of Memorial Day weekend, Alec, a good friend, arrived from the city, sparking a dual reaction in me, as he often did. After a sound hug and kiss on my cheek, his words smacked me between the eyes. I had barely sat down when he said, "So, how is your diet going?" My insides flinched at his words. Was I never going to get away from this subject? How often did I fear others asking that, yet few came right out with it. Alec always did. He was always frank, simultaneously accepting of me just as I was, so I felt I could be honest.

Tonight I didn't have the heart to go into it, but instead launched into a response triggered from my automatic defense system. "Well, I've decided to go at it slowly this time, really changing my lifestyle so I don't gain the weight back. I've only lost a few pounds. I joined Weight Watchers (but haven't gone in three weeks, I thought to myself). And, I'm having the best time walking and biking in the village (the rare times I had)," I babbled.

Stopping abruptly, I stared at the ceiling. To my ears, my explanation of the new understanding I had come to about myself sounded like excuses for not losing weight. It was an old story. I was always on some diet or other, so when I met someone I would subtly indicate that my weight was on its way down, certain this was the time I was going to lose weight. Then, inevitably, nothing happened. I would fall off the wagon and then be on edge waiting for the friend to ask why. I was embarrassed to have failed again. I'd kick myself for my lack of motivation and self-discipline.

Avoiding Alec's direct gaze, I again wondered if that was why I didn't stick with friends for long. They would see me repeatedly fail, and I couldn't face them. Or maybe I just couldn't face myself. It was easier to deny the problem than to face my failure. Then I looked at Alec, and something surrendered inside me. It didn't matter what he thought. I knew the truth. "The truth is that I've been trying to figure out why I can't make myself lose weight, why I can't stick to a diet," I said with resignation. "I feel like I'm making progress, but I'm afraid to say so or I'll jinx it."

I prepared myself emotionally for his response. But it wasn't what I expected. He smiled, his face softening, and said, "You know, Heidi, I like the look in your eyes this time. I think you're going to make it." My eyes clouded with tears as he patted my back. I looked at the floor and longed to believe him.

Memorial Day weekend came to Stonington with a bang; the number of cars and people tripled overnight. After that, the tiny town seemed to burst at the seams and put on a campish air. Elizabeth and Emily had guests most every weekend, and they often invited me along to dinner or a movie.

Until then, I had stayed pretty aloof from the singles group at church. But, in the flush of my new desire to reach out, I decided to go to a singles lunch one Sunday afternoon.

Walking in the door of a house in Mystic, I surveyed the group. A couple of perky girls in their early twenties chatted by the window with an older woman. I went into the kitchen with my donation to the dinner, a salad. At the stove was Melissa, the hostess, and at the sink a tall blond man I'd noticed at church. Melissa introduced me to the others. "Hans and I met briefly once before," I said, as we came to the blond man.

"Oh, yes, I remember," he said vaguely. Well, that's that, I thought. I immediately dismissed him, remembering that he had been only cordial when we met a few weeks earlier. I knew his kind. The good-looking guys always discounted me at first. Later, when thrown together because of circumstance, we often became friends. But, pretty face or not, they usually couldn't get past my being overweight on the first meeting. I had heard that Hans was an Austrian aristocrat who had recently bought the building across the street from where I lived. He didn't seem too personable, especially for a neighbor.

Two young guys were setting the table. There, without the potential for rejection, I felt comfortable. I went over and offered to help. Over dinner the whole group laughed and talked about everything, from politics to the local fishing fleet. At one point, when our conversation turned to my studies in Salzburg, Austria, Hans perked up. "What did you study in Salzburg?" he asked.

Anxious to impress, I rattled off the art, history, music, and German classes. "We had several professors with us from my college, but we also studied music at the Mozarteum Conservatory," I concluded. Within minutes we were tossing German phrases back and forth as we compared notes on Austria, a topic we both loved. He offered me a ride home, and, as we got to Stonington, we decided to take a walk through the village.

Over the next few weeks, Hans would often drop by without notice. I'd hear "Heidi," his European lilt coming through the window that fronted on the main street, followed by his steps coming down the side of the house to my door at the back. At first, it disconcerted me because I never knew when to expect him. I wasn't used to such intrusion into my privacy. I was afraid that he'd catch me when I wasn't dressed right, or more importantly, when I was in the middle of eating. Maybe not bingeing, but eating something sweet that I'd be embarrassed if he knew about. His visits interrupted the rigid routine that kept my life in control. But more often, I felt inclined to forgo that precision in favor of the warm feelings I got each time he or my new neighbors reached out to be with me.

ॐ ॐ ॐ ॐ ॐ

It was on a Friday evening in June, as a group of us sat around a huge wooden table playing Trivial Pursuit, when I finally realized that these new friends honestly cared little about my appearance. Hans had arrived a bit early to pick me up, so I hadn't finished sewing the button on the dress I was making and planned to wear. We'd been out all day, so I was sunburned and wore no makeup. I panicked at the thought of going out without the shield of being dressed just right. Then, in a defiant instant, I had put on a shapeless, sleeveless sundress. They'll just have to love me as I am, even with all this fat on my arms, I thought.

As we played the game, I kept looking for some sign that someone was repulsed, and found none. I saw only Hans's encouraging smile as I tried to come up with the answer to some obscure question, and Susan and John making cracks about how their team was going to win. These people actually like me, I realized, as warmth spread inside me. They didn't even seem to notice that I had no makeup on and that my bright red arms were almost twice as large as an average woman's.

That next Sunday my well-fortified walls crumbled a little more as Hans gave me a ride home from church. In my typical role as entertainer, I couldn't let moments pass in silence. I asked questions and recounted interesting stories. Yet that day as we drove over the vast New London Bridge, I suddenly stopped. I was so tired of being the one to entertain. I'd been feeling depressed earlier in the day, yet here I was, gushing good cheer as though I hadn't a care in the world. An image of Friday night came back to me, when my friends seemed to enjoy me whether I was chattering or not. Maybe I would try just being the way I felt. I looked out the window and was quiet for a change.

A few miles later Hans asked, "So, how is your work?"

Startled, I answered simply, "Fine. Another article, another day."

He prodded a little more. "What have you been working on this past week?" He was asking *me* questions, wanting to know about me. I wasn't used to it, but it felt pretty good. As I began to tell him about the article I'd been working on, I realized I'd been feeling frustrated because the details of the article were so complex. I told him about it and, surprisingly, the feeling eased.

"How do you organize a story on a technical topic like computers?" he asked.

"Well," I began, my automatic response being to portray an image of impeccable professionalism. But for some reason, instead I said, "It gets pretty scary sometimes. At first, I get overwhelmed with all the diverse facts that don't seem to fit together. And I wonder if I'm in the wrong profession." I finished with a sigh.

He nodded in sympathy and said, "I'm amazed you can do

it at all. I couldn't." Then he added, "I suppose we all struggle with work that is worthwhile." So this is how it feels to
let people in, I thought as I looked at his admiring face. It's
not so bad.

⊁ ⊁ ⊁ ⊁ ⊁

The second week of June, as the warm days of summer settled on the town, I was typing on a story when Elizabeth
knocked at my door. Delighted at the prospect of seeing her,
I was taken aback at her ashen demeanor. "What's wrong?"
I immediately asked as I drew her inside my apartment.

"I don't know quite how to say it. It seems like some horrible mistake." She hesitated, and then looked straight at me.
"Emily drowned yesterday when her ship sank."

An emotional jolt pressed me to the chair nearby. Just a few
days before, Emily had been enthusiastically telling me that
she would be part of a crew on a tall ship in a race from
Bermuda to the mainland. Now, I listened through a haze as
Elizabeth described how water had poured into the ship when
its masts broke in a storm. Eighteen other people, many of
whom had also worked at the Mystic Seaport, died along with
Emily. A bewildering pain settled over us both as we hugged
in silence.

Opening the mailbox later that day, I found letters ad-
dressed to Emily. I expected her to bound out of the front
door as she had that first day. Turning from the mailbox, I
smiled as I remembered her disheveled enthusiasm. She always
seemed poised on her toes, heading somewhere, ready to
plunge unafraid into something new. I thought of the way
she embraced life and people as I headed back to my solitary apartment.

Ironically, her death brought me to feel more alive than I had in years. I felt the need to convince myself I was a part of the living — to reach out and risk, to push past my fears of what others thought of my weight. Instead of waiting for the world to come to me and prove it liked me, I began to initiate get-togethers with friends and to be more open.

The next evening, as I was coming across the street with my laundry, I heard my name. I turned to see Hans. Rather than simply exchange greetings, I invited him to my house for dinner. Dropping off my laundry, I stopped upstairs to ask Elizabeth about going to Emily's memorial services the next day, and there met a couple of her friends who were visiting. I asked them all to join us for dinner. In minutes we had put together an impromptu picnic from the chicken they had marinated, salad fixings from my refrigerator, and Hans's offerings — a big bottle of Sprite and some dried fruit. We ate in the garden. Just before dinner, a quick summer rain shower cleared the muggy heat. As the sky cleared to fill with stars, we drew close in conversation.

It was such a stark contrast to a few nights before, when the self-loathing had come on me so quickly it was frightening. I had been watching television when the Jansens' son Paul knocked on the door. He was home from law school for the summer, his blond curls almost white and his skin deeply tanned from working outside with his dad. We talked a bit, then went out to the garden to join his parents, Elizabeth, and Emily's mother. In the course of the conversation, Paul invited Elizabeth to go out with some friends that Saturday night. He didn't say a word about me, I thought as I stood there. Feeling sure everyone noticed, too, and knew it was because I wasn't wanted, I turned to walk away. "We'll even take Heidi with us," he added as I moved away from the group.

All I heard in my mind was the echo of all the other times I had felt second-fiddle or was included because it was polite.

In disgust, I looked at how my stomach protruded, even in the billowy sundress I wore. I'll never be good enough as long as I'm fat, I thought. I kept walking. I got just inside my apartment before the tears sprang to my eyes. I was aghast that I could cry so quickly and intensely.

Leaving my apartment, I ignored their calls after me and headed across the street to the park. My anger turned inward as I walked along muttering to myself. "Of course he wouldn't want to be seen with you. What makes you think an attractive, intelligent man like that would want to be with you?" Suddenly I felt the desire to hit him, again and again, for all the other judgmental men I had known. He's a jerk, and his friends probably are, too, I thought. He can't even see that I'm better than women who have only a good figure to offer.

As I walked, I fought to make sense of my feelings and to reconcile my fat exterior with the idea that inside there could still be a worthy human being. Sitting on the bench in the gazebo, as I often did, I realized that before I had thought of myself as an extraordinary fat person. Though I may have been fooling myself, at least I had been able to face the world. These days I fluctuated between accepting the evidence around me that people liked me in spite of my fat, and being so repulsed myself by the shape of my body that I was sure everyone else was too.

After that, I began to see how grounded my self-image was in what I saw in the mirrors of others' opinions. I was confused because my new friends had no obvious need for me to fill. They didn't want to use my typewriter or expect me to play the listener. It made me nervous not to be able to see that they liked me because I provided some service. I cynically questioned their motives for wanting to be with me.

One night, after having dinner with Elizabeth and her parents, who were visiting, Elizabeth came down to talk.

"My parents thought you were terrific," she said.

Immediately I questioned it in my mind. I wanted to say, Be specific; what was it they actually thought worthwhile in me? But I realized she would think I was crazy if I asked that. Still, I wondered. If only Elizabeth could give me a list of the redeeming qualities her parents saw in me, I thought. Then I could understand how they used that to balance out the irredeemable quality of my obesity.

⋞ ⋞ ⋞ ⋞ ⋞

As the end of July approached and I made plans to leave Stonington, I felt tightly wound inside. Although I hadn't made a conscious decision to return to New York, it seemed I couldn't check out of life, as I put it, much longer. Sandra was getting married soon, and if I didn't move back I would have to find someone else to sublet my apartment. I also needed to get back to living in New York because my editors liked the security of having me a few blocks away. In all those months, I'd gotten only as far as writing an outline of my novel. Over recent weeks it had just gathered dust. It would have to wait.

I reviewed the past few months with mixed emotions. The weight was still there, but so much had changed inside. I didn't know how, but I sensed that the internal lessons of these last months would help me reach some final solution to the weight loss someday. I was just as certain that my time in Stonington was past. It was time to re-enter the world. I found I couldn't retreat to discover the meaning of life. Life only followed me, and it happened to me in spite of my best efforts at physical insulation. Ironically, I had tested what it felt like to live outside my protective shell. And, for the first time, the feeling of extending myself and touching other human beings was competing with my desire for food.

One Sunday a few days before I was to leave, Elizabeth and I had a party for our friends. We had had such fun planning it together, and now our little garden, which had held so much love and understanding for me, was packed with friends, just as Emily had envisioned. Paul Jansen brought over the barbecue, and we roasted hot dogs and hamburgers. A brother-sister feeling had developed between Paul and me in recent weeks, and we bantered good-naturedly as we prepared the food. I picked at the fresh vegetables and had a modest hamburger, but wasn't particularly interested in food. The conversation held my attention, and friends came by with farewell hugs. In the cool evening someone pulled out a guitar, and the melodies of old folk songs drifted by as Brian, Elizabeth, and I sat talking at the stone table near the rose bushes. I realized I hadn't been aware of my weight, or feared the judgment of others, for several hours.

Later, as I cleaned up the remnants of the party in my apartment, I could hear laughter from the few guests staying overnight with Elizabeth. One friend was going on to visit his girlfriend in Worcester, Massachusetts. Two others were heading home to Boston. Brian and Elizabeth were going to his cousin's on Long Island where they planned to relax, swim, and ride horses for several days. I felt antsy and unsettled as I washed the last of the dishes. Everyone except me had someone expecting them and somewhere to go. The threads of closeness and human caring that I had felt the past few hours were quickly unraveling. I was alone again, still unsure of how to permanently capture the elusive feeling of belonging.

Walking past the mirror in the hall, I started to avert my gaze as I usually did. But this time I stopped and studied *her*. That was how I thought of my body — as *her* — someone else, separate from the person inside, the person who was just like Elizabeth or Sandra. The dress I had sewn for the party suddenly looked silly. Look at the fat calves, the arms, the bloated round face, I thought. "I hate you," I hissed at the image. "You have denied me everything." My eyes dropped to the floor. I couldn't stand to look in the mirror anymore. Then, I saw the remains of the colorful cake Elizabeth and I had made. Half of it was left.

My next memory was of lying in bed, stuffed and sick at heart. The laughter had died up above. They must have gone to sleep, I thought. A pain flashed somewhere inside me. How could you eat like that again? Haven't you learned anything? What will it take?

I'll worry about it tomorrow, I thought, and slipped off into a sugar-drugged sleep.

CHAPTER FOUR

Another Year, Another Struggle

Fall 1984 — Fall 1985

From my idyll in Stonington, I went home to Colorado for several weeks; I visited my family and wrote a couple of magazine articles. Back in New York, I began working to create a life like the one I had begun to glimpse in Stonington, a life of opening myself more to my friends, of moving ahead in my career, and of getting control over my eating and weight.

As I walked into a singles social at church my first weekend back in New York, I warmed to see so many familiar faces. Vic, my husky blond pal, came running up. "Well it's about time you were back," he said. Just then another friend appeared with a camera. Inwardly, I cringed. Outwardly, I smiled, slid my arm in Vic's, and angled my body so that most of me was hidden behind him. It was a practiced position. Vic and I went on chatting until a pretty girl came bouncing up and laid a proprietary hand on his arm. My smile didn't waver, but a flash of memory brought a stab of pain. I remembered the time a few months before when I had helped Vic clean his apartment in preparation for a visit from a girl he had invited from out of town for a black tie event. Second best, was playing over and over in my mind. Second best. Good enough to clean up and kid around with, but not presentable enough to be seen with in public.

After the social, I grabbed something to eat at the deli and went home. In my apartment with my food and television I felt safe, but only for a few minutes. As I looked out my window at the lights of Manhattan, a hint of depression came in. No, I won't, I thought. I can control this. I won't slip back into old habits that harmed me before in this apartment — hopelessness, depression, isolation. I won't. I decided in Colorado the things I need to do to keep progressing and I will do them.

Mentally, I reviewed what I must do. First, be more socially involved as I did by going to the party tonight. Second, join Weight Watchers tomorrow before I lose momentum. Third, check on the YMCA down the block for an exercise program. I will control my life, I thought. The image of the perky girl with Vic came to mind. "I'll be like her. Give me one year and I'll be proud of how I look and at home with my body." I felt purposeful and determined.

A few days later I left church with Janna, happy to have time to be with a friend I had known since college and to get this chance to become closer. Then my feet started hurting. The weather was still hot and humid even though it was October. "Let's walk for a while," she had said, and of course I had agreed, even though I was squeezed into high heels and hose — a deadly combination for a 280-pound woman on New York's brutal and blistering streets. Within two blocks, my feet and hips were aching and my thighs chafed from rubbing together in the sticky weather. Hoping Janna didn't notice, I tried to keep from limping as I listened to her. The friendship idea was waning. I just wanted to get home where I could be comfortable. It didn't occur to me to simply tell her my feet were hurting and to ask if we we might sit down somewhere. She wanted to walk, so we walked.

My weight is in the way of my life again, I thought as we continued down Broadway toward Columbus Circle. How many times had I not gone with friends to a Broadway show because I was afraid I wouldn't fit in the seat? Even if I could wedge my fat body in, it would embarrass me by spilling over into their space. I was still mad at myself for not going with Vic a few days earlier when he was taking some visiting friends sight-seeing. When he mentioned it, my heart had jumped at the idea, but it immediately sank when he said they would be taking a walking tour of Midtown Manhattan. I wouldn't be able to keep up. And what if I got into some situation with a small chair where my weight would embarrass me? I turned back to Janna now, hoping my face revealed none of the physical and emotional misery I felt. I told her that I had forgotten about another commitment. "I need to head on home," I said.

As we parted, she turned down the block. I crossed the street and checked to see if she was far enough away not to see me board a bus only blocks from my home. As I hobbled into my building, I cursed myself and my body for ruining another opportunity for friendship.

That night I felt an irrational need to run someplace, to the window, to the roof, anywhere, as long as it was away. I couldn't breathe as I recalled how I had limped along Broadway that day, trapped inside my huge body. I remembered other times in the not-so-distant past when I had sat with friends and suddenly wanted to jump up and run out of the room screaming into the street and fresh air, away from the closed-in feeling that had overtaken me. Standing in my apartment now, I didn't know what it was I wanted to run away from — others or myself? It's a panic I don't know how to cope with, I thought. Perhaps the person inside can't deal with it so easily anymore — the restrictions this body puts on her, the restrictions the weight puts on her. More and more lately, I was faced with a horrible realization: I was hiding from the world and all the things that I was capable of accomplishing. All that is keeping me from happiness is myself, I thought. There was nobody else to blame anymore.

I resolved to change my attitude about myself and dove headlong into what had always made me feel worthwhile, my career. In November I got my first real travel-writing assignment that would take me abroad. I visited Yugoslavia with a group of executives who were considering holding conventions for their corporations there. Years before I'd figured out that travel writing was something I wanted to do. It was the best of all escapes — living the rich life without being rich, because the trips were paid for by someone else.

About a year earlier when I had first seriously investigated getting into travel writing, I was politely told by editors at the big travel magazines that I needed to get some experience before I wrote for them. Nine months elapsed before I had met the editor of *Successful Meetings*, a magazine for people who plan meetings and conventions. It was here that I found my long-hoped-for entrance into the field. With the Yugoslavia trip I began writing about how to arrange meetings for groups in exotic locales. Soon, I started being invited on press trips all over the world. This not only gave me the chance to travel but also to publish travel articles that would build my portfolio.

Sitting aboard a private yacht in the U.S. Virgin Islands in January 1985, I was certain I had arrived as a travel writer. I was on assignment for *Sales & Marketing Management* magazine to write about how companies charter yachts as a reward for their top-producing salespeople. The horror of the previous two days seemed a world away from the languid sunshine and fluttering breezes of the Caribbean. The assignment had come up quickly and I grabbed it, dropping everything at the thought of a warm escape. I had called two editors to delay deadlines, scrambled for cash to take along, although everything but incidentals would be covered, delayed paying my rent and phone bill, and dug through my closet to find something that resembled summer clothes.

I had rushed to get to the airport a good hour and a half ahead of time, because I had to be sure I got a window seat near the front of the airplane. Hurrying to the gate, I stood near the entrance of the jetway so I could be sure to be first on the plane. It wasn't until I was seated and sure the seat belt was long enough to fit, that I breathed a sigh of relief. Now, I would be saved the embarrassment of asking the flight attendant for an extension. Everything was all right: I was near the window so other passengers wouldn't see how large I was. I had unobtrusively put up the armrest so that if someone sat next to me, the person wouldn't likely go through the bother of putting it down. I couldn't fit in the seat if he or she did! Still, I was a little on edge and I hoped no one would sit next to me. Then I could put the center tray table down to eat on, saving me more embarrassment: my stomach stuck out too far for me to pull down my own tray.

But that was all yesterday, I thought now, as I shaded my eyes to devour the view of sparkling water and sunlight surrounding me, with the yacht anchored close to shore. Life was different here in paradise. My mouth watered as I spied a table laden with fresh pastries, bacon and eggs, juice, and fresh fruit. Only Harry, the captain, and Nicki, the first mate and our cook, were in sight when I had come out onto the broad back deck. The others on board, two affable couples in their late twenties — arrived a few minutes later, wearing bathing suits and shorts, the uniform for sailing in the tropics. What a luxury it would be to dress like that, I thought, as I looked down at my sundress. Shorts weren't an option for me because they didn't come down past my knees. Besides, I couldn't find any that fit.

After breakfast, one of the passengers casually asked if anyone wanted to go for a swim. I declined, pleading jet lag.

As the others dove in giggling, I envisioned being part of their world, a world where my choice to swim would depend on whether I felt like it rather than on what I looked like. I felt antsy as everyone fanned out to water ski, windsurf, snorkel, or lay in the sunshine. Here I was, on the edge of so much to do, but I could only watch. As my eyes rested on the slim lines of a bikini-clad woman lying on the bow, I suddenly realized what an odd image my hulking body would present in the same scene. It isn't a romantic picture, I thought, remembering how angry I had often been when a man couldn't think of me romantically. A hint of understanding struck me. I was a little less righteously indignant at the men of this world, who from childhood are given skinny heroines to put into their romantic fantasies, just as I had been.

By mid-morning, with everyone busy with their own pursuits, the boat was quiet except for Nicki, who was working in the galley. Having surveyed the scene and finding that no one was close enough to see me, I slipped out of my sundress and into the clear, bright water off St. John. I quickly forgot about my ratty bathing suit and misshapen body, wholly taken up by the wonder of this new experience. Without worrying whether anyone was watching my body, I splashed and dove freely. A school of minuscule yellow fish swam up close to me, a curious one following me almost onto the beach. I watched in fascination as a green-and-red-striped fish played in the pool of water near the beach. As my body floated on the surface of the water, totally at peace, my mind slid into a comforting, numbing, blank abyss.

Throughout the rest of the week I stayed on deck in a sundress, taking my secret swims when the others were off on some adventure and spending the rest of my time eating the delicacies left out for snacking. Nobody seemed to notice how much I ate, because a vacation atmosphere prevailed —

everyone was indulging. I did venture out once when we stopped at the Baths on Virgin Gorda, going ashore by dinghy to the massive rock formation that formed caves and pools of water. But as we loaded into the dinghy from the yacht, I almost retreated. I knew I was the size of two people and that the tiny six-person boat would shift alarmingly when I stepped in. Could it hold me? It was too late. Everyone was waiting, and watching, so I stepped in. Once ashore I started toward the Baths with the others, only to realize, even at a distance, that I couldn't fit between the rocks. I made an excuse about being claustrophobic and returned to the beach to wait until it was time to go back to the yacht.

I returned to New York on Saturday and continued in my dream world through Sunday, basking in the warmth of comments about my tan and telling people all the glamorous details of the trip. But by Sunday evening, the depression I felt at facing reality was unavoidable. I couldn't ignore thoughts of all the fires I sensed were burning in the stack of mail and the phone messages I had yet to confront. Not knowing was worse: I prayed that the checks I needed to pay the phone bill and rent had arrived. Some had. One hadn't. That meant calling the magazine in the morning, and risking having the editor think I must not be very successful if I always needed to get paid right away. Well, the damage hasn't been that bad on this trip, I thought. At least no checks had bounced. There were various messages from friends and editors. Why don't they just leave me alone? I wondered as I prepared for bed.

The next morning, reality fell on me like a ton of bricks. But my mood brightened at the thought of the trip to Monte Carlo that was only two weeks away. I wasn't about to give that up, so I dug into the articles I had left in various stages of completion. Between running down to the basement with loads of laundry, I edited one article and began to make phone calls for background information on another. By early afternoon I had switched to binge mode and was watching television as I ate a stack of pastries. But that's okay, I told myself, I always get a second wind in the evening. The next two weeks went on like this, as I rigidly focused on work and sleep — subconsciously scheduling midafternoon binges of cookies and cake after a lunch of burritos or hamburgers.

I followed my mid-afternoon binge with a nap. Then came a four-hour work period before my evening binge of pizza, pastries, and potato chips, accompanied by television.

One night Janna called to ask whether I wanted to go to a movie. "I'm just so busy," I said with a sigh, as I went on to enumerate all my different assignments. "And I'm trying to get out of town week after next, heading for Monte Carlo," I said, hoping to sound casual rather than pretentious.

"How was your last trip?" she asked. "You were so lucky to get out of cold New York for a week."

"It was great," I answered, flipping into automatic. "The yacht was outfitted to snorkel and windsurf, and we swam," I said, pushing down the uncomfortable feeling that I was letting her believe I had snorkeled and windsurfed. I did swim, I thought, wryly thinking back to my solitary interludes.

"Listen, you need a break. Why don't we do a movie tomorrow night?" she insisted. Picturing my precisely laid out day of working and eating, I felt shaky at the thought of spending an evening with her. I couldn't be sure when I'd be most creative. What if the urge to work came and I wasn't near the computer? Taking three hours off to go out with Janna seemed impossible as the pressure about my unfinished article built up. But she seemed to really want to go, and I'd let her down so many times.

I said yes and fully planned to go, but the next morning I awoke feeling hungover. I had binged again, and the sugar dulled my brain. But I got up early anyway, ate a healthy breakfast of cereal and fruit, and was at work at the computer by 9:00 P.M. By eleven, I was already contemplating what time I would go out for lunch, and whether I wanted pizza or the oversized hamburger and french fries at Goldies. I decided on the hamburger, and after eating it I went on to a couple of slices of cake and some cookies. At about three, I called Janna, panicked. The writing hadn't gone well, and I was desperately hoping I'd be able to focus for a few hours that night. "Listen, I better work," I said, feeling guilty for canceling yet again. Work never quite materialized that night. I sat in front of the television with a bag of Doritos and dip all evening.

ॐ ॐ ॐ ॐ ॐ

Returning from Monte Carlo ten days later, I felt confident that I had covered my bases better than I had before going on the Virgin Islands trip, but there was one bombshell I hadn't foreseen. It was a messy corner of my life that I had effectively denied for three years now.

I picked up my mail when I got home from the airport, and now I sat numbly looking at an envelope with a return address from the Internal Revenue Service. I thought of all the times since I started free-lancing that I had gotten my paychecks and barely had enough to pay rent and buy all the deli items and fast food I "had to have." I wasn't quite sure how I was supposed to be handling taxes now that they weren't automatically taken out of my paycheck, but some part of me had long feared that it would finally catch up with me. Here it is, I thought now, opening the letter to find that, indeed, Uncle Sam wanted to know why I hadn't filed a tax return for 1982. "I'll deal with it next week after I get over these immediate deadlines," I assured myself and put the letter with my stack of bills. Over the next few years, as other notices came, a clinch would come in my stomach and then my mind would shut off. I didn't know what to do, so I did nothing, living in terror that someday someone would come to take me to jail.

By the spring of 1985 I was traveling at least one week out of every month. As a contributing editor for *Successful Meetings* magazine, I often represented the magazine on trips when staff editors were unavailable. Once I could show the big-name magazines that I had published travel articles, I began to work on assignments for them too. Many of the public relations people who arranged press trips also had gotten to know me and now sent me on trips, hoping I would write about their location for the travel magazines I worked with. Once I got inside the travel writing network, the process was easy. In fact, I was turning down trips. I began a frantic lifestyle of traveling to some exotic location, then rushing home to write an article on it. I'd do my laundry and keep my personal life somewhat active, then I'd run out of town again.

In March, when I was asked to cover the opening of a new Florida resort, my immersion into a fantasy life of travel suddenly forced me to face reality again. On that trip, the inner Heidi was unmistakably faced with the reality of the outer Heidi. The assignment had come at the last minute, and again I rushed to get an extension on deadlines for several articles and had finished others while I juggled my cash flow. After having worked long and hard all week, I needed comfort, and the luxury resort perched on the white sands of Florida's Gulf Coast felt like Camelot.

I arrived on Friday afternoon, a few hours before I was scheduled to attend a cocktail party to meet officials from the resort as well as the other writers invited on the trip. Starting on Saturday, we were to tour the hotel and local sights throughout the weekend.

As we lounged around sipping drinks after lunch on Saturday, I suddenly noticed a man videotaping us. "What's he doing?" I asked everyone in general, as I straightened up and angled sideways so I was partly hidden. My worst suspicions were confirmed: he was chronicling our weekend for a presentation on the last night of the trip.

I spent the rest of the weekend on the lookout for him, praying his tape wouldn't be too damning. Wait, I thought to myself at one point, whatever they see on tape can't be much worse than what they see of me from moment to moment. It was then that I realized that facing them wasn't what I feared. No, it was my precarious self-image that was in danger. It was the picture I had of how well I presented myself, which allowed me to show up in these groups rather than shrivel away in embarrassment, that I was worried about.

By the time they showed the video, my fear had swelled to enormous proportions. Everyone laughed chummily as snippets of our trip ran past on the screen. Appalled, I was frozen as I watched a bloated, misshapen woman with pale skin and unkempt hair. She seemed foreign to me. In recent months I hadn't bothered with makeup as often, and didn't have time to sew clothes, so I was left with whatever I could find to wear. That isn't me, I thought. It revolted me. I closed my eyes. It was too painful. Then, in morbid curiosity, I opened them. The being before me looked neuter, more a round blob than anything resembling the female form. There were familiar bits and pieces to her eyes and gestures. Still, she seemed to be light-years away from the image of myself that I carried around in my head.

As the movie ended, a deep, inescapable understanding settled over me: the woman I had seen on the screen was really me. I looked up in wonderment as an amiable woman turned to me. "Wasn't that funny, what they pulled together for us?"

she asked, as several others joined us. How could she treat it so lightly, acting as though she actually liked me? The others made comments about their own frailties as they invited me to join them for drinks. I was genuinely confused. How could they even stand to talk to me, let alone be so friendly, considering the revolting image I presented? I was even more perplexed with how my friends in New York saw past this horrid body and accepted me as a friend.

For two days after I got home I couldn't seem to motivate myself to work, and I didn't leave the apartment except to get food. On the second evening I sat alone, surrounded by empty packages and wondering what was wrong with me. "I can't seem to muster the enthusiasm for diets anymore," I muttered to myself. Remembering the image on the video, I felt untouchable and unworthy as a human being. Tears dropped from my glazed-over eyes onto the packages around me. I had stuffed myself until I was sick, and still I felt this pain. I couldn't get my brain to turn off. Why? I used to be able to.

A few weeks later I still hadn't shaken the image on the video, but my total rejection of the person I'd seen was slowly turning to tolerant acceptance. By April, when Janna invited me to a California beach party at her apartment, I realized something positive had come from the horror of the video. Something had happened inside me when I saw myself on the screen. I had had to face what I was projecting to the world, and I began to make peace with the two parts of myself — my inner and outer selves.

As I took the bus to Lane Bryant the day of the party, I realized that I had bought few items of clothing over the past couple of years, as my weight ballooned and my money shrank. But no more ignoring my body and depriving it, I thought as I entered the store, which was full of colorful clothes in large sizes. Surely I would find something here. A few minutes later

I had actually found a festive flowered dress that looked like one I had seen in *Glamour* magazine. I smiled at my image, feeling almost normal. I was so happy to find something that fit and was in fashion. Over the next hour or so my spirits rose as I found several more outfits that actually fit.

Dressing for the party that night, I couldn't believe how much fun it was to have these clothes and to feel like I was chic and looked good — for a fat woman. I felt like a new woman: I wanted to lose weight, and I was beginning to like myself in the process of becoming what I wanted to be physically. I realized I was making peace with the inside and outside — accepting my obesity, which didn't mean I planned to stay that way.

As I dressed, I realized that before I had rejected my exterior, pretending that I was projecting an image other than that of an obese woman. If I had faced the reality of my true weight before, I thought, I wouldn't have been able to function. Now, though, acceptance, but not complacence, was my new attitude.

When Vic arrived to take me to the party, I felt some part of the inner Heidi shining through. "Hey, dude, look at my boss shades," he kidded as I opened the door. Then he added, "You look great. Red is your color."

౨ఠ ౨ఠ ౨ఠ ౨ఠ ౨ఠ

The next week found me in the midst of a serious effort to change my weight and shape, and especially my attitude. They all fit together, I thought. I can't expect to change one without changing the others. On Monday morning, as I walked to my Weight Watchers' meeting, I made my way at a determined pace through the enticing smells of pastries and pizza that fill New York's streets. Eating is always on my mind, I thought. Only, now, instead of eating when I'm bored, depressed, frustrated, or lonely, I'll analyze *why* I want to eat. It's usually out of habit or because I want to soothe negative feelings, I reasoned. I'd heard in Weight Watchers that losing weight was about changing behavior. That made sense. So now, when I wanted to eat, I'd do something else instead: go for a walk or maybe knit a sweater — just focus on something else.

At 290 pounds, I found it hard to picture myself thin, yet I seemed obsessed lately with finding a hint of the cheekbones I had when I had weighed 230. I couldn't picture myself thinner than that. I'll just control my exercise and food, and the weight will come off, I told myself. Even the struggle of staying on Weight Watchers was better than not doing anything. At least I felt like I was being a good girl so God would be with me. Only when I have done everything I can should I expect God to help me, I thought.

All of these decisive actions I was taking began to make me feel more in control, and also freer, and I called Patrick to begin therapy again. We established a payment schedule that I could afford.

Two weeks later, all my good intentions were folding under me again. Baffled, I tried desperately to make sense of why I was sliding off Weight Watchers. I'd stopped weighing and measuring my food a few days before. Now I sat with pretzels in my hands. I'd already downed a dozen. Well, it isn't really sweet stuff like doughnuts or candy, I rationalized, but some part of me knew sweets were only moments away. It won't help to beat myself up, I thought. Okay, logically, what is going on? Why do you want to eat this? I started to review happy and sad events of the past few days, but ended up finishing the package of pretzels instead. I didn't give in to sugar that night, but the next day I did, eating an entire bag of chocolate cookies. Depression and lethargy set in. I was so weary of this tired, bloated feeling. I knew that when I used food to kill feelings, it didn't last. Why can't that realization be enough to make some huge change in my heart automatically? I wondered.

As my soul struggled on, my writing career burgeoned. Focused on my next trip, I could forget my resounding failure in dieting. Then one morning I was watching "Good Morning America" when the actress Meg Tilly was being interviewed. Her words stopped me in my tracks as I was fixing breakfast. She said, "You can't put your heart and soul into a career because in the end it will betray you, if that is all you have." It is all I have, I suddenly realized. In the past year I had almost completely pulled away from friends with the excuse of running off to some wonderful location. And there was no man to love. Would I ever have a family? Then an image of Vienna at Christmastime came to mind, bringing with it excitement at the thought of my trip to Austria and Hungary in a couple of months.

Through the autumn I began to question my perceptions of friendship and love. My friendship with Doug, a handsome, blond, athletic California boy whom I met soon after he arrived in New York, caught me off guard. Our relationship started just like many others I had been in, where I was drawn to the nurturing he provided and instinctively understood and provided what he needed so I could become indispensable in his life. I immediately started helping him with his job search — anything to spend time with this confident, relaxed man who, to my delight, obviously enjoyed being with me. He was always at my place, having dinner or typing his résumé on my computer. Then we'd sit for hours as I talked through many of my fresh pains. He'd talk about the latest girl he was dating. The way he described them, I knew he'd never be interested in me, and I accepted from the start that we would be nothing more than friends.

The usual resentment emerged, along with my fear that he

only wanted to be my friend because I helped him. Then one night I began to understand the nature of friendship in a deeper way. Doug phoned me just as I came in from a party. I was feeling confused and depressed but I wasn't sure why.

"Hi, I just thought I'd call before I left work. How are you?" he asked.

"Okay," I said hesitantly, feeling needy but not wanting to sound like it. "Do you want to come over for dinner?" I continued, figuring I had to offer something for him to want to see me. But he seemed to hesitate.

"Well, I don't know. I always seem to impose. Do you want to talk? You don't sound so great." I wasn't sure, and said so, but he heard it in my voice. "Listen, you don't have to fix dinner; I'll be right over."

After he arrived, we sat on the couch while I talked and cried about how my life wasn't working. It was because I couldn't lose weight. "You know, Heidi, I think you put too much emphasis on your weight. You can do whatever you want," Doug said sincerely. "Plenty of A-plus people are overweight. Maybe you should just accept it and quit fighting. Go on with life." As he left with a revised résumé in his hands, I smiled to see that my typing his résumé was nothing next to the spontaneity he was teaching me and the trusted, listening ear he offered so readily.

My growing — and authentic — friendship with Doug made me examine the discrepancies that existed in my relationships with other men. One night as I was having dinner with Scott, a guy I did things with periodically, I wondered about the gray areas I so often found myself in with men. Were we dating or just friends? My relationship with Scott existed in limbo: we went out but never had any physical relationship to define that we were dating. As Scott cooked dinner for me at his house, I looked at this good-looking law student before me and felt I should be grateful that someone like him thought I was worthwhile. As we sat down to eat, he commented on how fun and interesting I was, and I began to believe that he thought I was worth caring about. I loved having someone doing all he did to make the evening right for me. How could I not like him? I wondered. I remembered Janna saying she was going to go out with Scott, and suddenly I wanted to see him again. There was the ever-present fear of being usurped by another woman. It never occurred to me to think whether I wanted to be involved with him.

A few weeks later Scott and I spent a weekend exploring the New England fall foliage. Just after sunset on Sunday, we stopped for a bit at Stonington Lighthouse point. The moon shimmered over the water, outlining the breakwater and islands on the horizon. As I breathed in the salt air, I sighed at the memories of the time I had spent here. Looking at Scott in this romantic setting, I suddenly realized I felt only friendship for him. I cared, but I didn't want more, no matter what he wanted. It was a startling realization to see I had a choice. To me, if a guy had all the outward signs of what I wanted, he had the power to accept or reject me. How could I not be interested in someone who is a law student, holds the same values I do, and is nice looking and personable? I wondered. Then, with a pleasant start, I realized that I didn't have to be romantic with either Doug or Scott. I liked being with both of them just as friends.

๕ ๕ ๕ ๕ ๕

Tucked in a worn wooden booth at Chumley's a few nights later, Doug and I couldn't stop laughing. I had brought him here, to my favorite restaurant, a charming old renovated speakeasy in Greenwich Village, to celebrate his birthday.

"Okay, okay, so this is what happened." He continued his story about the exploits of an art director at the advertising agency where he had just been hired. Then the conversation turned to the woman he had left out west when he moved to New York. They had finally decided to marry, and I was happy for the shy sparkle this commitment brought to his eyes. Watching his animated face, I felt grateful for our closeness over recent weeks and all that I had learned. I was also a touch sad at the inevitable shift his engagement would bring. Of course our friendship would remain, but the texture would change.

As Doug finished outlining his plans, he picked up his birthday gift — a sculpture of a sea gull in flight, representing his wonderful future — and we headed home to watch a movie on television. Saying good night at the elevator a few hours later, I wondered whether to hug him or not. I was afraid that my fat body would repulse even my good friend, but I wanted to give him a birthday hug.

"So, happy birthday," I said, taking a couple of tentative steps toward him.

"Thanks so much, Heidi. You're a true friend. I don't know what I would have done without you these first months in New York," he said, giving me a resounding hug.

"You're not such a bad friend yourself," I responded warmly. Waving as the elevator doors closed, I headed back into my apartment with a new perspective, the nurturance of his hug and words lingering with me.

CHAPTER FIVE

Crumbling Fortress Walls

Fall 1985 — Summer 1986

One Thursday evening early in November 1985, a man entered my life who would become a dear friend and who would lead me further toward recovery. A friend gave Greg my name, suggesting that he call me about a writing project he was working on. Greg had done extensive research for a book on management styles and entrepreneurs and now wanted to make it marketable. He called to ask if he could take me to dinner to bounce his ideas off me.

The afternoon of our dinner meeting I thought of canceling, again feeling pressured by deadlines and afraid of meeting someone new, but when he showed up at my apartment I was glad I hadn't. It was clear we thought alike when we discovered we each owned the same model of funky old Kaypro computer. We spent an hour chatting and playing with the computer before we went out for dinner, where the similarities in our lives and perspective became more apparent. We were both the middle child of seven siblings and had studied and traveled in Europe. As he talked about his family, it became apparent that he had sisters who battled with weight. He seemed sympathetic but didn't dwell on the topic. He seemed to see past my weight to the inner Heidi I so wanted others to see.

As we walked home, Greg hugged me, saying how glad he was that we had met. I smiled and agreed, but was surprised that my fat body didn't seem to inhibit his affection. He was tall and handsome, with light brown hair and intensely warm blue eyes. He worked as an analyst for a prominent financial company where his intelligence and wit were obviously an asset. Men like that were always friendly enough to me, but Greg's demonstrative and genuine warmth from the outset was something new for me. Several times that night he had touched me, either squeezing my hand or putting his arm on the back of my chair as we talked. I felt cared for, and surprisingly, I wasn't afraid of touching him either. His ready smile of appreciation held no hint of expectation that I would have to change in order for him to care. I felt totally accepted, by his words and touch. It was an odd feeling.

Closing the door after we said good night, I felt lighter than I had in a long, long time. Happy even. I felt as if God had guided Greg into my life that evening for a reason, if only to show me that for that evening I was touchable and lovable.

From the first night there was never a hint of judgment from Greg about my weight. My highly sensitive radar would have picked it up and made me pull up my emotional fortifications if there had been evidence of any. I began to see more of Greg over the next few weeks. I suppose I was infatuated with him from the beginning. Although I didn't really know what love was, something brightened inside of me at the thought of seeing him.

We saw each other all the time. He lived only two blocks away, so he would often call or simply drop by after work. The panicky voice inside of me always reminded me that he would never be interested in me as a woman and told me not to get my hopes up. But I kept trying to balance this voice with the one that told me to enjoy the way I felt around him and not to think about the future. Part of the thrill of being with Greg was just knowing that I was capable of feeling a lift of spirit and that there were men out there to whom I was drawn.

Emotionally and quite literally, Greg burst through my defenses before I knew it. He jostled my orderly little daily routines by showing up unexpectedly and suggesting some escapade. I felt I should expect him anytime, but didn't resent it because I wanted to see him whenever I could. Yet I couldn't count on a solid block of private time at home in any given twenty-four-hour period anymore. There was no more hiding from the world, no more escaping. Greg wouldn't let me. But then I didn't feel that I needed to hide myself much. I had begun to test my boundaries of trust with Doug, and now with Greg I felt a readiness to open up that I hadn't experienced in years. He pushed past my assumptions about men and my self-protective devices to show me he just plain liked being with me. It was refreshing, and because he often told me in words and through his touch, I began to trust him.

About 10:30 one night a couple of weeks after we met, I was curled up in my nightgown when the buzzer rang. The doorman said Greg was on his way up. I rushed to get dressed, my hair in disarray and my face without makeup, while he waited in the hall.

"I'm sorry for just dropping by," he said with obvious embarrassment as I opened the door to my tiny studio apartment.

"No problem," I said laughing, "as long as you don't mind waiting in the hall sometimes so I can get dressed."

He nodded in agreement and handed me a paper bag. "Here. I come bringing a party," he said. Inside was a bottle of tonic water, a can of Tab, and a lemon. He'd brought us drinks just like those we had ordered a couple of nights earlier. Cutting the lemon, he prepared the drinks and sat on the couch to talk.

Greg's habit of showing up after running, or calling at the last minute to see if I wanted to go to a movie, made me less self-conscious about expressing my desire to be with him too. A few nights later, I called him. I had just finished an article and remembered his suggestion a few days earlier to call if I ever needed a break from work and he'd do the same. "I'll come by and throw a pebble at your window," he'd added. "Well, more like a piece of cement. It might be tough to find a pebble in Manhattan."

And so, I didn't hesitate to call my new pal and ask if he wanted to go for a walk. When he answered the phone, he said he was just thinking of heading over to throw a piece of cement at my window. As we strolled through a nearby park, we stopped every few yards, intense in conversation. He seemed to want to know me, how I thought and felt, and that surprised me. I wasn't always the one asking the questions and keeping the conversation going as I had done with other men friends. Before, I had written scenarios with a particular man in mind, adding the appropriate feelings for both the man and me to have. But this night was different. This night Greg and I really did touch hearts. He talked about his family and how it had been growing up with an alcoholic father. I told him about my brothers; about Thomas's mental retardation and Michael's death. We talked about lighter things too — college and our adventures in Europe. For once, reality was better than fantasy. As we parted, Greg said, "I'm so glad you called."

I answered, "I'm so glad you were going to throw a piece of cement at my window."

A week later I realized Greg was not only bringing out the fun-loving side of me, but a deep caring side that I had squelched for years. He'd had a rough day, so after dinner at our favorite Chinese restaurant, China Garden, we came back to my apartment so I could massage a knot in his back. Feelings of tenderness and empathy washed over me as I remembered the things he had done for me. I finished by massaging his forehead, recalling Patrick's words in our session the day before. I'd told Patrick I felt a strong caring for Greg and that I didn't know whether to give in to it or not. He responded with, "You've locked yourself up and been afraid for so long. Why not take a risk and share the feelings? What could happen to you that's worse than what already has? You've been hiding out from feeling for years since Tom, only caring for men on the surface." I couldn't define my feelings for Greg except as a deep caring. I decided to relax and have faith that it would all work out.

Getting up off the floor, I didn't feel the old wariness because of my size or the need to control what Greg thought of me by moving a certain way or even by diverting his attention by talking. I smiled to myself as I realized how happy I was becoming with myself, just the way I was. Yet ironically, it didn't mean I didn't want to lose weight. Rather, it just gave me a different, more realistic, perspective. I wondered if this was the acceptance that Patrick had said he thought I needed before I could lose weight. It felt so good to let go of the image I had of myself as a wounded animal, which I had had since Tom ended our relationship. I didn't even have the desire to talk deeply about the past as much anymore or to dwell on the injustices of my childhood. I had begun to let go. I felt worthy of the good life I was enjoying.

Still, Greg couldn't completely quell the waves of insecurity and confusion that kept slapping at me. The next time I massaged his back, a few days later, an entirely different set of feelings surfaced. As I sat down on the carpet to give Greg a back rub, he pulled off his shirt so I could rub on some lotion. To freely caress him was at once relaxing and frustrating: I was ministering; we weren't physically involved in something together. At that moment all logical thought and patience went right out the window. I just wanted some clear-cut indication that I was a woman to him, not just a friend. The back rub sent only half signals — touching, but not eye contact. Do friends act this way? I wondered. I didn't know. I was so mixed up about men that I didn't know where to draw romantic boundaries. I felt like I was missing part of the script.

Do I really think he could be physically attracted to me? I asked myself as I turned off my feelings and massaged his back. I knew the turmoil in me wasn't about Greg. Why did this struggle burn inside me so much, insistent and yet eluding identification? It was the search for a man who would accept and love me totally as I was — overweight. Was it as simple as that? No. The man who did love me would walk into a trap, a trap built by my own conceptions that I was worthy of love only with a thin, unmarred body. No other body was acceptable in my mind. Nothing I was or did made up for not having it. Yet I had spent my whole life trying to make up for it, to prove to the world I was just like thin women and could get everything I wanted in career and romance without losing weight.

⚓ ⚓ ⚓ ⚓ ⚓

Just after Thanksgiving, when I went on assignment to Budapest and Vienna, my eyes were opened, and I began to see that others saw me in a different way. In Vienna, I visited Maidi, an old friend of my mother. Waiting to see the Vienna Boys Choir perform one morning, Maidi and I clasped hands as we talked. As usual, within the first few minutes I had slid in a comment about being in the process of losing weight. I felt like her granddaughter as she turned to me and said, "Don't lose too much weight, because I knew someone who did, and she got real bitchy. You have such a lovely personality it would be silly to ruin it." I smiled and agreed, but thought to myself that there was no way I wasn't going to get skinny.

Maidi insisted that I read a letter she had given me to deliver to my mother, so as I packed before leaving, I pulled it out, sat on the edge of the bed, and read. "Heidi is herself a sheer delight. I do need gentleness and a peaceful being like hers to feel confident," the letter said. I put it down with a rueful laugh. This is so far from who I feel I am these days, I thought, with this anger raging inside so much of the time.

As I put the letter away I realized Maidi truly saw me that way. I have to accept that I do have a good part that is compassionate, I thought. Yet I have such trouble accepting it as real. Perhaps this is the spontaneous caring part of me that Patrick said I should let out with Greg. It's so much easier with little old ladies like Maidi, I thought. But I'll try to learn not to be frightened of letting it show. The words Maidi used were what people had said about me in the past. I shouldn't discount it now. Despite my doubts about the accuracy of Maidi's view of me, it brought joy to my heart to read it. I felt that maybe God was pleased with me, and I needed to know that.

Finishing my work in Vienna, I stopped for a couple of days in Salzburg before returning to New York. As I wandered around my college haunts one afternoon, my mind shifted focus from the excitement of traveling to the feelings inside me. It was the first quiet moment I'd had to myself on the trip, and feelings of frustration and depression welled up in me. These feelings seemed to come rumbling to the surface periodically. Or was it that when the flurry of my life settled momentarily, then my emotions finally had a chance to surface? Either way, it is a familiar and grim cycle, I thought: after weeks or months of focusing on some exciting project, the moment inevitably comes when I am alone with this pain. The reality of how I felt in relation to my body and what I was going to do about that reality was such a burden.

My sigh deepened as my appreciation of the view of the palace gardens surrounding me gave way to some stunning realizations. It doesn't matter how many Dougs come along, telling me that plenty of A-plus people are overweight and that I have a choice of losing weight or becoming a healthy overweight person, I thought. Or people like Maidi, who actually tell me not to lose the weight. In spite of the Dougs and Maidis of the world, and the apparent caring of the Gregs and Scotts, *I* am miserable with my overweight body. Just me. None of the positive feedback I get from others penetrates the barrier surrounding me, the barrier of how I feel about myself. Nothing is enough. I'm not good enough while overweight, yet I seem powerless to take the obvious next step and lose weight.

Walking on, I stopped to sit on a bench along the Salzach River. And now, I thought as I watched a sea gull swoop close to the rushing river, I face in Greg someone I think I could enjoy spending my days with.

For all the fluttering and fun of being with Greg, the feelings in my soul told me two things. First, even if Greg could love me in spite of my weight, I would never believe and accept it as real. I would find fault with his loving me and discount his worth over time because I felt that anyone who could love me as I was wasn't quite up to snuff. The second reality that came to my mind was the fear that the potential for love was there with Greg, as it had been with Tom, but it would never evolve because I was fat. It's all so early with him, I thought, shaking my head as if to reorder its contents. It felt good to know that with Greg I wasn't projecting or fantasizing a man's interest in me.

His presence, and his obvious appreciation of me, created questions I had never faced before. He could take one of the jobs he was considering in Seattle and be gone from my life. But really, that doesn't matter as much as the fact that it's the first time I've come to this crossroad, I thought.

122

For the first time in years I saw that what I truly wanted might be out there somewhere. I can reach for it, whether it's with Greg or someone else, I thought as I shifted on the bench where I sat. But I have to make some choices because I can't live the life I want with an overweight body. I saw in front of me a clear choice of two lives. I could continue to have spurts of excitement in my life, followed by depressing periods when the little girl inside of me rose to the surface and said, I'm not worthy of the good life, and it's easier to hide anyway. Or I could choose to consistently feel good about myself by becoming physically and spiritually healthy — by keeping the link with God clear.

I suddenly realized that my own internal battering was what kept me from a fulfilling relationship with a man and from greater closeness with my friends. Somewhere along the way the negative habits of hiding physically and emotionally that I learned during the years I had spent on the couch with my knee problem had become normal for me. It was a shock to realize that I had come to believe those habits *were* me. I think that I am a bad person because of my weight and my isolation, I thought. But my weight and isolation aren't the essence of me. I can separate them from my worth as a person.

How remarkable, I thought, feeling a deep understanding ease into me. It isn't that I'm unworthy, but that I ate and isolated myself to cope as best I could with my childhood. Now it's time to clean up the mess and move on, so I can grasp the future with both hands. I need to learn to cope in positive ways, stripping away the habits and ways of coping that I used to get me through a tough period. Changing these habits will be a slow step-by-step process. As slowly and unobtrusively as they crept into my life as a way of dealing with problems, they can leave. I felt an amazing sense of lightness as I realized I wasn't fighting to change what I had come to think of as my dark soul, but was really uncovering confusion to reveal my true soul. I had felt the essence of Heidi when I was helping Maidi in Vienna. A voice inside had said, This is you, Heidi. Take it in. Peel off the layers and discover your divine nature as a daughter of God.

ℳ ℳ ℳ ℳ ℳ

In the weeks after my return from Europe, I began to feel more comfortable with myself as a woman. Friends began to comment on the change they saw in me, and I noticed it too. I was surprised at how differently I perceived my image one day when I saw myself in the audience of a "Phil Donahue Show" I had visited. My, I thought to myself, who is that pretty and vivacious, though obese, woman on the screen? My perception was validated when a friend called to say how beautiful I had looked and asked what had happened. I told her that some shifts had been taking place inside me in recent months. I had lost a bit of weight, but that wasn't it, I realized. No, it was much more than losing weight. My spirit felt lighter.

What people saw was an extension of the healthiness that was growing inside. A sense that a part of me was returning, or was in some way awakening for the first time, came in all areas of my life. In an editorial meeting at *Successful Meetings* magazine one day in early January 1986, the editor referred to me as a columnist and contributing editor. I really heard it, and for the first time actually accepted that I was an adult and a career woman. Feeling more like a woman than a school-girl, I began to dress like one. I wore makeup more often and shopped in Lane Bryant stores for professional outfits. I suddenly began to see myself as a success, rather than as a struggling free-lance writer who never quite got what she wanted.

That afternoon, as I left my office at *Successful Meetings*, I felt a nagging fear emerge that it was Greg's caring that had made me blossom. I thought that without it, I might return to my former self. But I realized that he was only one part of the growth. Our relationship — his unconditional acceptance and support of me — had made me want to take emotional risks that had had a ripple effect in other areas. I felt more confident in trusting my instincts, asserting myself in choosing topics for my column, and considering where I wanted my career to go. Greg hadn't let me down, in large part, because I hadn't set it up so that it would be possible for him to, as I had in past relationships. I was realistic about what we had and recognized the friendship as valid, whether it turned into a romance or not.

By the end of January, Greg and I had decided to become partners in writing his book on entrepreneurial management. Walking through Central Park one snowy Sunday afternoon, he asked me the question that had been on my mind since we first discussed the idea of us working together. "Do you think the book would interfere with our friendship? I don't want it to do that. And I don't want you doing it just because we're close. I want you to do it because you believe in the idea," he said with the pointed sideways glance of a friend who knew I might agree to work with him just to please him.

"Oh, no, I think it would be wonderful to work together," I said without hesitation, ignoring the pestering fear that I was saying yes to make sure we would continue to spend time together. Instead, I focused on how much fun it would be. I warmed at the memory of the night before, when I sat curled under his arm on the couch as we looked at some of the edited manuscript. It had felt so relaxing and warm, so secure. At the time I thought, This is the way to write a book.

Of course we would do it. Was there ever any question? It meant everything to Greg, and I wanted him to be happy — I truly felt it was a good project. I saw so much in him that

I didn't think he realized. And I was impressed by his research and findings. We communicated so well that I was sure it would work out.

Within days, we slipped easily into combining the professional relationship with our growing friendship. Working together came naturally. One night, as I sat at the computer, Greg walked back and forth behind me, talking through the cover letter we were composing to introduce our book proposal to publishers. "Let's open it by explaining that this research is the first done and . . ." His voice trailed off into thought as he absently came up behind me and began rubbing the tenseness out of my neck and shoulders.

Relaxing under his touch, I responded. "That would be okay in the next paragraph, Greg, but we really need to start with something punchy to catch the reader's attention."

Thumping me lightly on the head, he said, "Not a bad idea, Heidi Ho, let's try that."

Grabbing a pad of paper and pen, he motioned me to the couch as he scribbled some thoughts. Over the next couple of hours we pounded out a rough draft of the letter, then headed to China Garden for dinner. "That's what is so good about how we work together," Greg said as the waiter set down our food. "When we don't agree we say so, and then we are able to work through the questions," he concluded, and we dug into the steaming mounds of chicken and Chinese vegetables.

In February, Greg got a definite offer for a terrific job in Seattle. He told me one evening as we sat in Keats, the cozy little pub near my apartment that had become a favorite haunt of ours. "I just don't know what to do," he said, truly pained at choosing between the lifestyle and city he had grown to love and the prospect of the ideal job for him.

I'd known there was a possibility of his going, but with it right in front of me feelings poured through my heart. Ignoring them, I flipped into my good friend mode. Help him get through this, I thought, shutting out all consideration of the effect his choice might have on my life. I'd deal with it later. "Well, will it further your career to go out there? Could you come back to a better job in a few years?" I asked in an appropriately objective tone. We went on to talk about the pros and cons logically, as I pushed down my own feelings.

Later, at home, I wasn't at all detached. Tears fell as I prayed that Greg would be given wisdom and insight to make the decision that was right for him. But part of me also wanted God to somehow control the situation and make it right, make Greg not leave. "I'm so confused," I said out loud as I half knelt and half sat near my couch. In recent months I had begun to feel less and less like a victim of my life, and more like I had control and could make choices to change. "But then I'm hit with how truly powerless I am over some things and people, and I don't understand," I prayed. "Your will. My will. Greg's will. How does it all fit?" I wanted to talk Greg into not leaving, to exert the influence I knew I had as his closest friend in the city, but I knew I couldn't. And that was what made me feel helpless. I knew I had to be a true friend and objectively help him make his own choice, no matter how it would affect my life.

Despite bracing myself emotionally, it was still a crushing blow when Greg decided to take the job. One night, after we had discussed it for a long time, I knew inside it was best for Greg to go, but I didn't want to accept it. I didn't want to lose what we had, what he had given me. We stood now saying good night at the door. "Well, I guess it feels right for me to take the job," he said, sounding relieved to have finally decided.

I halfheartedly smiled. "I agree. It sounds like a wonderful job," I said without even considering what I might be feeling.

Then Greg went on to talk about getting together on the weekend to work on the book. I felt a flash of pain and then anger. I wanted to slap him, to do something dramatic to bring him to his senses about leaving — to withhold working on the book as some sort of blackmail to make him stay, or to scream at him that, by leaving, he was ruining his life. But I stood quietly, only half listening as he went on talking. My mind jumped to all the other times when I had begun to feel close to a man and something happened so that he left. The nurturing never stays, I thought angrily. In that instant, I wished I'd never met him.

"Well, good night," I said abruptly, drawing in emotionally. He seemed hurt and surprised, mumbling good night and turning away as I started to close the door. "Wait," I said, something melting inside me. Our friendship deserved more honesty and openness than that. "I think we better talk some more." And we did, about how frightened we both were of growing closer over the next couple of months before he left, only to feel more pain at parting.

ა ა ა ა ა

Only a few days later I was off to Athens on assignment and to an experience that would more deeply draw my body and spirit together. Realizing Greg was leaving had put our relationship in perspective. I had allowed myself to merge so fast with his problems and enthusiasm for his book that I hadn't taken time for myself. Now, as I headed out of the deep winter snow of New York and into the sunshine of the Aegean, I sensed that my wholeness had to begin with me. In Athens, in the anonymous, solitary, and plush Inter-Continental Hotel, I began to uncover parts of myself I had denied all my life because I was fat.

One afternoon, having completed the interviews I needed for the article I planned to write, I had a massage. As I arrived in the health club, the masseuse handed me a large towel and a pair of thongs and told me to take off all my clothes. When I gingerly walked into the massage room a few minutes later wearing only the towel and thongs, she told me to lie down and pulled off my towel in one motion.

I'm naked and she can see me, I thought, in mild shock. The ripple of fear I felt about how disgusted she must be suddenly halted. What the heck? I'll never see her again, I thought and laid down on the table. I tensed as she methodically massaged each part of my body. But once I detached from my inhibitions about how ugly she must think I was, I came more closely in touch with my body than I ever had before. I shut off the judge and let the accepting sensual part take over.

By the end of the hour, I was beginning to feel a new abandon. It was a small health club, with a Jacuzzi, sauna, and steam room. There was something freeing, invigorating, and sensual in dropping my towel and walking nude into the marble steam bath. As I eased onto one of the long slabs, I marveled at how out of touch with my body I was. I'm always running from one piece of clothing to another, I thought. Not ever facing myself, let alone letting anyone else see me. For so many years I have disassociated my body from the essence of me, I thought ruefully. But lately I've begun to feel like a woman. I own all parts of me.

No one was around, so I stepped over to the tile Jacuzzi, dropped my towel, and went in nude. The water jets punched my sore stomach and thigh muscles lightly. I felt as though I had never acknowledged them as parts of me that I could shape and take care of. I wanted a fit body with fluid lines. Today, as the masseuse worked on me, I had felt or seen a picture of an athlete. I wanted to make those muscles she rubbed truly worth a rubdown. But that would demand an awareness of my body that I didn't have yet.

Dressing in front of the mirror a few minutes later, I looked at my nude body, not terrified as I had been before of the image I presented. It's coming along slowly, I thought. And it's easier to accept it, knowing I can change it. Before, I had focused only on my head and shoulders, ignoring the rest of my body in a desperate attempt to maintain my confidence. But the reality is that the *whole* body and the *whole* soul are together. I had ignored and hidden from bits and parts of myself, both spiritual and physical. That night, as I exercised to a Richard Simmons tape rather than ordering room service, I felt as though I was gathering together the fragmented bits of my body and soul.

*   *

Greg quit his job the first of March so we could spend a month developing a solid book proposal before we tried to continue the project long distance. I decided to put aside my magazine work for a few weeks and focus on the book. That month, although he was living in Brooklyn, Greg spent virtually all his time at my apartment. He brought in his computer, and we set up our two computers back to back on the table so we could both work. We fell into a pattern of him sleeping on my floor each night and of the two of us working all day together. We meshed together perfectly. I was amazed that I didn't mind having someone that close to me all the time, twenty-four hours a day, except for showering and his occasional treks to Brooklyn. We plowed through the book proposal single-mindedly, lost in our world together. We'd found a joint passion.

I told friends I couldn't see them while I worked on the project, and I didn't miss them. When Greg and I did take a break, we'd take a walk or go to a movie or dinner together. Our lives became the management book. As I worked with him on this project I found for the first time that I was capable of making a commitment to a large undertaking and following through. It was exhilarating.

During that month food wasn't an issue. The urge to binge had magically subsided. Enthralled with this man and his passion for the book, I lost my appetite. I was getting all the nurturing I needed from him, so I didn't feel the need to binge. I never felt lonely or afraid because I was so involved with him. Greg was a healthy eater, only occasionally over-indulging, as most people do, so I fell into his pattern of eating. I ate what he ate without thinking, feeling satisfied with what we ate and sometimes skipping meals entirely. Just by pick-ing up his habits of eating and walking more, I lost about ten pounds that month.

But the desire to binge returned toward the end of the month. Greg and I had been together for three weeks nonstop, and I was beginning to feel claustrophobic. I'd made excuses during the past week to run out on errands alone, picking up a Hostess pie or bag of Doritos to scarf down before I headed home. On Friday I found myself encouraging him to head to Brooklyn to pick up some more clothes. As soon as he agreed it would be a good idea, my mind started planning what food I would get. First, I'd stop at the deli for a ham and cheese sandwich with lots of mayo and chips and then drop by the bakery for some pastries. Would they still be open at 7:00 P.M.? I wondered. Telling Greg vaguely that I needed to "pick up a few things," I left the apartment with him so I would have more time to binge before he got back. Once I was sure he was headed the other way to the subway, I crossed back and ducked quickly into the bakery. When he returned, I was lethargic from a sugar overload and terrified he would smell the sweetness on my breath.

Working with Greg had been a haven of denial, but that all ended during a four-day visit to an old inn in Vermont — our reward after working hard to finish the book proposal. On the surface it was a getaway as we slept, talked, toured the area, and ate. And ate. We were both eating nonstop, and for the first time Greg felt like a binge buddy. He made no judgments about my eating, saying nothing about my choices. So I ate what I wanted. Well, mostly. It was certainly more than I usually allowed other people to see me eat. We'd get up and have a big breakfast, take a short drive or walk, end up talking on the bed, take a nap, eat lunch, nap or read and talk, have dinner, and go to bed early. We were both regrouping after a month of intense stress, but perhaps also escaping our fears about the book we'd just dropped off with a major publisher.

On our third day there, after a big lunch, Greg was napping on the bed as I sat by the big window that ran from floor to ceiling under the eaves of the inn. It was a perfect scene, the snow piled up on the sidewalk and an antique horse-drawn carriage parked on the cobblestone street. I was writing in my journal, trying to put down in words the extraordinary experience of letting someone really know me. It was the first time I'd been with someone and felt I could be whoever I was. I'd always been so sure my private habits were weird and so different from other people's that I had thought I would have to hide them or at least modify them.

Things had been different with Greg, partly because of the difference in me, and partly because he demanded that I be totally open and then accepted whatever that demand brought from me. In fact, Greg liked who I was. I would sometimes hesitate to say just what I thought or felt, and then I would boldly do so because I knew it was safe. It seemed such a simple thing, but my past fears of saying what I thought were still strong.

As I sat writing in my journal I realized that I could not help but feel an enormous gratitude to the man who slept nearby. I thought of the night before when, as I got into bed, Greg had come over, joking about tucking me in and patting my cheek before getting into his own bed. It was sweet, and somehow the sweetness had tugged at my heart. Then a feeling of desolation washed over me: Was he just another man who could feel only friendship for me? And why did friendship, which is a great gift, make me feel so worthless?

Before I knew it, tears were pouring down my cheeks in the darkness of the room. Trying to keep my crying quiet, I considered walking outside so I wouldn't have to explain. We'd talked about so much, but this corner of pain was mine alone. I had no intention of telling him what was wrong, because I thought it would affect our relationship and push us into a discussion of intentions.

Suddenly, Greg's voice broke into my pain-filled thoughts. "Are you getting a cold?" he kidded in a tone that said he doubted it. "I hear sniffles over there." When I didn't answer, he went on gently. "Heidi, are you okay? I can't sleep if I know something is upsetting you."

After a couple of minutes I simply asked him if he would hold me. He jumped up to come and lie down next to me. But he wouldn't let me be. He kept urging me to talk; cajoling, threatening, caressing my arm until I began to wonder if maybe I should let it out. I searched the ceiling, looking for a way to say something. Of all people, he was the one I most trusted and cared for. Even so, I thought it was impossible to talk about what I was feeling. How could I admit my fears of being left for a thinner woman, of inadequacy, of never being good enough, and most deeply, of being untouchable and unlovable because I was fat? It was too ugly a corner to expose. I would feel crushed if he turned away from me. I blushed in embarrassment at the thought of his knowing I felt that way, that I was so vulnerable.

Somehow in the dark of the night the words came more easily than I thought. As I lay close to him, he encouraged my trust and everything came out bit by bit. At times, tears streamed down my cheeks. I felt anguish at expressing fears to someone who meant so much to me. First, I spoke of never feeling good enough. It wasn't the deepest part, but it was all I could get out. I said, "I never felt good enough, could never be good enough, because I was . . ." I couldn't finish the sentence. I couldn't actually say it.

"Because you were what?" he asked.

I answered, "Overweight."

He sat up quickly as if startled. "You are? I never noticed. Why didn't you tell me?" he said in mock horror.

I laughed at him then, beating him with the pillow. "I should have known you wouldn't let me take myself too seriously," I said.

In that simple action Greg told me all I needed to know. His humor conveyed total acceptance and the subtle message that my weight didn't bother him that much. It was crucial for me to hear that. He soon returned to bullying me to continue talking. Little by little I opened rusty doors, letting out feelings and thoughts that had been imprisoned for years. Greg just listened, smoothing my hair. By my expressing them and his so openly accepting them, my fears seemed to lose their hold on me. Greg didn't try to refute those fears or call them silly, nor did he say they weren't reality. He just acknowledged what I felt, telling me in word and touch that, of course, I was lovable.

As my emotions stilled, we talked more logically. "It's good to let that stuff out and have a reality check," he said.

"Why didn't you just tell when I first asked?"

I squirmed a little and then answered. "I was afraid you would think badly of me; that you would see me as someone who doesn't have confidence. That isn't exactly the image of me I want you to have. I was afraid you'd think you had hooked up with a loser."

After assuring me that he thought nothing of the sort, he added, "Besides, Heidi, you can't ever control what I, or anybody else, thinks of you anyway."

But that was something I always tried to do, with everyone: I tried to keep up the image that my fat didn't bother me and that I was a winner, full of positive energy and success, hoping others would see me that way.

It was quite a night, I thought now as I finished writing in my journal. My eyes returned to where Greg slept. Conflicting emotions filled me as I watched his dear form breathing. The intense memories of the past month, when we'd grown to depend on each other even more than in the months before, flooded my consciousness. How could I think of him being totally out of my life in only a couple of weeks? I began to slip into the role of heroine in one of the romance novels I read, hoping to gain some distance from the simple, sad pain I now felt. But the distance I wanted wouldn't come. I'll go for a walk, I thought.

As I walked through the massive wooden door of the inn out into the snow, my feet carried me down a side street. I should be crying, I thought. I should be trying to get in touch with my feelings. Nothing came. My mind felt numb as I crunched along the tree-lined streets in the snow. I was headed in no particular direction. At least I thought I wasn't, until I found myself in front of the pastry counter of a little country store. Some part of me had been heading there since I had left our hotel room. Guiltily, I grabbed two oversized cookies and a doughnut, paid for them, and headed back outside. Reaching my hand into the bag, I looked at the surrounding mountains, trying to take in the beauty. Instead I focused on the food. I ate and walked in the snow.

At breakfast on our last morning in Vermont I ordered a ham-and-cheese omelette. As I lifted the salt shaker, intending to put some on the omelette, Greg playfully grabbed the shaker from my hands. "Whoa, you're using too much salt. It's bad for you," he said. "It's just as if I saw a close friend smoking and knew it would hurt her," he went on, playfully defending his intrusion.

"I think that's my choice," I bit back at him. It was so unlike me. I wanted to punch him, my angry feelings flaring instantly as I envisioned Mother trying to control my food. Of course he had no idea of the inferno he had sparked, and we sat there for a few minutes in an emotional standoff. I looked down at the eggs, trying to understand what I was feeling. I wanted to please him and not cause friction. I thought of all the meals we had eaten when I used salt and he hadn't said a word.

But anger was only part of it. It was a territorial issue too. I'd kept my reserve up about my weight so well that it wasn't a topic even with long-time friends like Janna. Greg seemed to sense where those boundaries were, and then he took a step just beyond the wall. Some part of me knew he didn't buy the image I had worked so hard to project to others. I knew that he saw the inside that I tried to hide and that he liked me anyway. But this was as close as he'd gotten to my taboo subjects. I had let him in by expressing my vulnerabilities. But he was getting too close, taking liberties no one ever had in talking about my weight and food. I didn't know how to react. Finally, I was calm enough to speak. "You're right, Greg. Now let's eat and head on back to New York," I said, pushing down the feelings with practiced ease. Within an hour the incident was forgotten and we were singing to the radio as we drove through the snowy countryside.

❧ ❧ ❧ ❧ ❧

Within a week after we returned to New York, Greg left for Seattle. Reality hit me in the stomach with a sharp thud. My best friend was gone. In a way I was glad he was going out west, because now I could get on with dealing with the problems that kept me from my own happiness. The relationship with him had crystallized my deepest desires for myself and my future. Whether with him or another man, I knew I couldn't go further in a relationship the way I was. It wasn't only because I felt physically inhibited and unattractive, but because my weight and health at times had kept us from doing things together. As we had driven past a ski area in Vermont, I longed to be flying down the slopes, but of course I couldn't at three hundred pounds. On the many sailing and seashore trips I took on assignment, I didn't arrange for Greg to come along because I couldn't let him see me in a bathing suit.

The first few weeks after Greg left, I binged and hid out. When a two-day depression kept me from working, I recognized old habits and felt as though I were a hairsbreadth away from staying locked in my apartment. I sat staring at the wall, appalled that this could be happening again when I had made so many changes in my attitude in the past six months. I have everything, I thought, looking at the exciting life I led and wondering why it didn't seem to make me happy.

My world went along much as it had before Greg came into it. It was filled with press conferences, editorial meetings, drinks with editors, frequent travel — all edged by almost daily calls from Greg. The reality of it *was* exciting and fast-paced. Only, the excitement wasn't enough anymore. Knowing a bit of intimacy and warmth, I was greedy for more. The phone was totally inadequate for maintaining a relationship. I had seen a touch of what could be in my friendship with Greg and wanted it with someone. Yet now I had to put aside any thoughts of that kind of relationship with a man and go on with my individual growth. I was confused about what I felt for Greg, but I realized it didn't matter until I found myself. I knew I had to identify who I was and what I wanted and move toward it.

Working on the book with Greg had taught me the value of patience and diligence in reaching a long-term goal. I realized that I could commit and keep going on the day-to-day grind of developing my career and losing weight.

I resolved that May would be a month of big accomplishments. I made up lists of the articles I would write and the magazines I would contact and also planned how I would go about losing weight. But I woke up May 2 and couldn't face the morning. I simply couldn't go on with the day as planned. I wandered the darkened apartment, lay in bed with the pillow over my head, or ate chocolate cake. These actions were foreign to the "new" Heidi, but my brain was turned off. It wasn't me, yet it was.

Two and a half months later, despair permeated every corner of my soul as I sat in a park near my apartment in the stifling heat of a New York July night. I couldn't stay on a diet for more than a few days. Exercise hadn't stopped my bingeing, nor had it eased the inexplicable sadness that weighted my soul most days. There were few people in the park, so I gave way to the hopelessness and desperation that consumed me. Where always before I had thought I could control food and lose weight once I set my mind to it, I was despondent to find I couldn't control it at all now, even when I wanted to. Something much deeper is wrong, I thought. But I didn't have a clue as to what it was.

CHAPTER SIX

The First Faltering Steps

Spring 1986 — Spring 1987

It would be almost a year before I would actually begin to recover from compulsive overeating, but my odyssey had begun. My plan in the spring of 1986 was to pull up my bootstraps and get to work. My motto became, "Just grit your teeth and do what is best for you." I'm a strong person, I told myself, and when I want something badly enough, I'll work to get it.

So, with my chin set at a defiant angle, I swept past my terror of what others thought of my obese body and marched through the doors of the Vanderbilt YMCA to sign up for a fitness class. I had decided to take a different tack on dieting. I would exercise to increase my body awareness, believing that this way I could sneak up on losing weight. I would work on my food, sure, but I was certain that it would come naturally through my increased body awareness. I remembered the time I had taken aerobics classes for a month — my desire to eat had plummeted and my spirits had soared so high after each class that I ate only yogurt. Here was the key, or so I thought.

After another failed attempt at Weight Watchers, where I discovered my weight had climbed to 330 pounds, the highest it had ever been, I decided to try a support group program for people with eating problems based on the Twelve Steps of Alcoholics Anonymous. I'd seen a sign for the meeting, held each Monday night at the YMCA, on my way to the fitness class and thought it might be a good adjunct to my exercise program. Maybe they have a better diet than Weight Watchers, one I can stick to, I thought as I walked in. I vaguely remembered a visit I had made with a friend to a similar meeting the first fall I arrived in New York six years earlier. It had seemed like a glorified therapy session, where everyone sat around talking about their feelings instead of how to modify their eating behavior, but something drew me back this time. Besides, I thought wryly, knitting and going for walks isn't keeping me from the Twinkies.

As I walked into the cavernous room, I noticed a number of chairs set in a circle and a dozen people milling about. Only a few were fat, I noted. Good, that means this thing works. They're probably on a maintenance diet. I sat down, feeling uncomfortable and wondering why I was there. My discomfort increased as the leader began reading from the Alcoholics Anonymous Big Book, a text that the group used in the program of recovery from compulsive overeating as well as from alcoholism.

I don't have anything in common with an alcoholic or an addict, I thought huffily, but I stayed anyway. After we read a chapter from the Big Book that explained how to identify yourself as a substance abuser, people began to talk about their experiences with bingeing. Their words struck a chord deep inside me. Some were anorexic, others bulimic, and still others binged periodically and then obsessively exercised to keep from gaining weight. Yet they all talked about food in the same way.

Their words caught me. Their experiences were just like mine, but they said they were addicts, and I just *couldn't* be an addict. No, that couldn't be. Not me. Tears welled up in my eyes as I turned my focus to the bit of sky I could see out the window. But I continued to listen. A woman I couldn't see, because by now the crowd had tripled, was talking. She recounted how her binge had lasted the entire previous day, as she ate large quantities bit by bit. I got an uneasy feeling. "I'm so tired of feeling like that piece of cake has control over me, so tired of feeling fat," she said. But I have my food under control, I thought. I eat pretty much normally, I just can't make myself diet. Certainly, I don't eat compulsively, I thought.

As she continued to speak, I thought nervously of a night several weeks back when I had done something I had never done before. Only a couple of hours after I had gone to bed, I got up — still almost completely asleep — and went to the kitchen for cookies. I opened the package and sat on the edge of the bed devouring its contents before going back to sleep. Listening now to people talk, I wondered what was going on inside me that I would do such a thing. Was I in such deep distress that my mind wasn't even conscious that my body had taken over? I've been fooling myself, I thought. I've buried my ability to observe so deeply that I don't see how blatantly out of control my habits are.

The speaker's words punctured my reverie. "I tried Weight Watchers and other diets, but nothing worked. I'm so sick of my body, yet I can't get away from how big it is when I look in the mirror."

She understands, I thought as I shifted so I could catch a glimpse of her. But she's thin, I realized, looking at her size-eight figure. Still, her attitude about food and her body was identical to my own. "It isn't even so much what I do or don't eat, it's my crazed attitude toward food," she said.

Yes, I thought, I definitely use food to satisfy other than physical needs too. And like her, I knew I'd had my last go around with Weight Watchers. It worked for people who had discipline, but obviously I didn't. I just couldn't stick with it anymore. My most recent try had lasted only a few days before the insistent cravings and excuses began and I caved in.

I realized then and there that I needed to be in this room, and I was determined to use the Twelve Step program along with my new exercise regimen. I wasn't quite sure what the Twelve Steps were, but they said something about admitting I was a compulsive overeater and asking for help from a Higher Power. I believed in God. It just never occurred to me to ask God for help to lose weight. It seemed like a little problem I ought to be able to handle if I were a good girl. The program would also force me to look at the problems that had caused my food addiction and to clean up my past. I knew I would have to make internal changes and reorient my entire life away from food. At that moment, it seemed the only way.

In the following weeks I kept going to support group meetings off and on, but I was still focused on exercise as my salvation. The day after my first support group meeting, I found myself juggling my schedule to find time for an exercise class, rather than making excuses why I couldn't exercise. As a result of sticking with my exercise program, I felt more control in other areas of my life, especially where my career and finances were concerned. Instead of letting others' thinness and my fear of their snickers intimidate me, I focused on doing what I had to for myself. Rather than constantly making excuses for not doing my best, I began to go all out, sticking to a tough exercise routine no matter how difficult it was. Although I'd been acting like a victim, I realized now that I had caused much of the pain I experienced in my career and finances by not doing a thorough job — by turning in slipshod assignments, failing to plan, and refusing to budget. Seeing this, I was determined to make a wholehearted commitment to exercise.

For the next week I hung on for dear life, exercising daily and refusing to binge. It was more than the fitness that drove me; it was keeping a commitment and doing my best at something. It was crushing to face that I had never done that in my life. Mostly I had made halfhearted efforts to merely get by, using standards set by someone other than myself. When I looked behind me at the trail of unfinished or tarnished projects in my wake, I felt physically sick. I had always looked for the easy way out. Now, I had to keep the commitment to prove to myself I could succeed. I toughed it out through classes where my legs cramped and my muscles ached as they strained to carry my massive weight.

Only eight days later, it already seemed like an eternity since I had made the commitment to exercise and stop bingeing. I wanted time to pass quickly, yet it seemed to move in slow motion. I was aware of each day's passing and of my focus on food. That eighth day, horrible cravings for sugar were followed by fatigue, depression, and discouragement. I want food as in the past, I thought longingly. But a strong core kept me from bingeing. If I stick with it now, I will only have to go through this torture of withdrawal once, I told myself. I had read somewhere that if you do something for thirty days straight it establishes a habit. And I was determined to succeed.

২৪ ২৪ ২৪ ২৪ ২৪

After my first support group meeting, my heart was open and I listened intently. But then, at some point, something inside me rebelled, and I bolted emotionally, unable to accept the idea of myself as a compulsive overeater. It was easier to focus on exercise than to think of myself that way. Two weeks later, I hadn't gone on an all-out binge, but I was still eating far more than I should. I went on with my fanciful life, playing my part as a writer in Manhattan and distancing myself from people at the support group. Then, I began making excuses for missing exercise class. Before I knew it, I wasn't going at all. How had it happened? I didn't know.

I dabbled in the Twelve Step program for the next several weeks, sitting gingerly on the fringes of the group and springing for the door as soon as the meeting ended. I couldn't face that I was one of them, couldn't come around to committing to working the program they said I must in order to be rid of "my weight problem," as I called it. They talked of desperation; I didn't feel it. Yet I couldn't stay away. Occasionally, the idea took hold in me, and the old "motivated" Heidi would rear up. "I'll do it!" — the conviction would rise in me, and I would think about the program's philosophy. Mostly, though, I thought of the program as being much like Weight Watchers — a nice pat little addition to my exercise program. But the people in the meeting spoke of drastically changing their approach to life as the only way to recover from this illness — an illness much like alcoholism. Their attachment to food was so profound that it made their lives a mess.

My mind balked at the idea. I denied that I was as bad off as others at the meetings. I just needed to lose some weight. I didn't want to go to the meetings, yet I was drawn to the truth I heard and felt there. I didn't want to talk to anyone or share in the meeting, and I couldn't say the words *compulsive overeater* about myself. At meetings, it seemed all I heard was people talking about bingeing on an entire half gallon of ice cream at a sitting. That wasn't me. And I didn't pick things out of the garbage either. Well, not very often, anyway. And only so I didn't waste food. I just liked my sweets, and even then, I could cut them out whenever I wanted to. I'd shown that with Weight Watchers. I just didn't have the patience to stick with it or a thorough understanding of why I ate. And I couldn't relate at all to those Twelve Step members who stuck their fingers down their throats to vomit the food they had just eaten; nor could I relate to a person who compulsively *didn't* eat.

Those were pretty insane actions. I just ate more than was good for my body, that's all.

୪ ୪ ୪ ୪ ୪

A couple of months later, Greg arrived for the Fourth of July weekend and New York's special celebration for the Statue of Liberty's centennial. I understood we were just friends, but in the months we had been separated, I had clung to him and the relationship as though they would give me happiness and help me avoid difficult realities. I was thrilled with the intimacy we had developed and amazed that he cared for me as deeply as he did. I was so thrilled that I often let it carry me away and take the place of dealing with myself. Thinking about him, talking to him long distance, and being with him when he came to New York on a business trip kept me from myself and the pain inside.

Slowly, I began to realize that overcoming my food problem had to be the center of my life now. Nothing in my life would work until I dealt with it. I finally realized that even if I lost weight, I would still be obsessed with food. Spending Liberty weekend with Greg was fun, but the relationship was not as encompassing as it had been before. It didn't work as a fix anymore: being with him didn't let me forget the realities of my life.

As we watched fireworks burst over Manhattan, I thought of a moment a few weeks earlier when I understood that even if a perfect romance with Greg were possible, it wouldn't make me whole. I had been standing on a balcony surveying the exotic lushness of Hawaii, where I was on assignment, and my thoughts had drifted to Greg. Things would be perfect if we were in love and he were here, I thought, as I picked a bright red hibiscus blossom. But then I realized that even if he were here, it wouldn't shut off the pain inside me. I looked at the beauty around me and saw plenty of people to do things with, yet I felt lonely. Then it hit me. I was lonely because I wasn't whole. There was an empty spot in me. Until it was filled and I was made whole, I would never fully connect with other people and I would continue to feel alone.

After Greg left, I began to see more clearly that I was a compulsive overeater. The only way out, I realized from my attendance at the Monday Twelve Step group, was to realize that as a compulsive overeater I had no control over food; it controlled me. Then, I needed to surrender the pretense of control. On a minute-by-minute basis, if need be, I had to turn to a Power outside myself for help in keeping from bingeing and in keeping from the thoughts and actions that led me to binge. Suddenly I was amazed at the crazy, self-destructive things compulsive overeating had made me do and think at times. I was shocked to realize that some hidden, unconscious part of me could actually entertain the idea of passing up a new life of growth, change, and happiness in order to obey my master — food. More than ever, I was seeing how my perception of the world made me unhappy, and how it stemmed from my obsession with food.

And, seeing that, I thought I could turn my obsession over to God's care, but I was wrong. After a day of talking myself into eating what I should, I suddenly found myself contemplating what I would binge on later as I watched Janna make a peanut butter sandwich before we went to a movie. One moment I wanted to slap it out of her hand; I was so angry with God that I could never eat like a normal person. The next moment I saw how starkly crazy my attitude was and how serious and pervasive the issue of food was in my life. Yet, even as I realized that, I clung to the thought that I could someday eat like a normal person.

As Janna and I parted that night, I realized I wanted control of the food, and the obsession, back. All my life I thought I had been so good about giving my life over to God, yet I saw now that I hadn't. In some odd way, I was even trying to control God — asking God to give me what I thought I needed in my career, friends, and finances. Asking God to grant me wishes like Santa Claus, rather than asking what God's will was for me. My whole life had been about control, yet I'd only discovered it in the last few days as I tried to truly hand control of my eating over to God. Intellectually, I could let go and trust God to take away the compulsion to binge, but another part of me wouldn't give up the idea that I could handle food. Some part of me still thought all I needed was the right diet or greater psychological insight.

A few nights later, even as I sat chomping on cookies, I read the Big Book and thought how similar my attitudes were to those of the alcoholics the book described. I have to begin to accept that I am a compulsive overeater and turn toward recovering from the addiction, I thought. Fascinated by the alcoholics' stories, I read for hours; I couldn't seem to absorb enough of the book. I found hope in the idea that there was a way out of the horror I felt at being out of control in every area of my life from finances to emotions, work, relationships, food, sleep, and daily habits. With God's help and the tools of this program, I can turn off the obsession with food, I thought as I closed the book and went to bed.

❧ ❧ ❧ ❧ ❧

In September I went to my first Twelve Step meeting of a group of people with all addictions, not just compulsive overeating. It was held in a little Connecticut town about an hour north of New York City. Many of the same people who attended the Monday night meeting came here as well. The group had a strict no-nonsense approach that food abuse was an illness, and you didn't play games with it. Instead, you followed precisely what the founders of AA did to recover — you worked the Twelve Step program. In fact, you grabbed it as though you were drowning — because you were — and you relied on a Power greater than yourself to recover. In this group I found my first sponsor, Diana, who had herself worked through the Twelve Steps. In her role as my sponsor, she would help me do the same.

A woman from the Monday meeting had said her roommate would pick me up at the train in the Connecticut town and give me a ride to the meeting. The person who picked me up was Diana. As I got into the car, she asked what had brought me to New York. I started in on my normal prattle about my career and travel, which usually impressed people. But with Diana it sounded hollow. I was embarrassed and stopped abruptly, sensing that she wasn't impressed.

"So why are you in this program?" she asked bluntly. At first I was affronted, but it was actually a relief to know that she didn't care about my facade; she cared about the real state of my life. I didn't have any idea how to actually tell her my feelings, or about my struggles with food, so I mumbled something about wanting to lose weight and was quiet the rest of the trip.

As I was about to board the train back to New York, Diana told me to call her if I wanted to talk. Her penetrating eyes were softened by a slight smile. "Really, call anytime," she said.

I said thanks in an offhanded way, my pride solidly in place as the "together" Heidi who was working the program.

A few days later, I thought of Diana's kindness and serenity when I was caught in the grips of another binge. Although her honesty had scared me, it was also a comfort. I felt touched in a place no one had ever reached before. Remembering that night, I cried because it felt so good to think that maybe

I didn't have to keep the facade in place any longer. Someday, I hoped, it would be gone forever.

I called Diana. She said she would sponsor me.* From then on, my days were spent in unfamiliar emotional territory and filled with things I didn't want to do. I began to feel I wasn't the same person at all. Unlike alcoholics who can swear off liquor for the rest of their lives, as a compulsive overeater, I had to face my substance three times a day. The only way to abstain from compulsive overeating was to strictly adhere to a food plan and learn how to eat healthily. I also needed to learn what a portion was, and to do that I was to weigh and measure every morsel that went into my mouth.

From the start I had to "turn over" my food, planning what I would eat for the day's meals and then calling Diana to make a commitment to follow that plan. I was then committed, and I couldn't change anything unless I called her to okay it. That was so my addictive mind wouldn't stay obsessed with food throughout the day, dwelling on whether to have turkey for lunch when I had committed to having tuna. The only times I could change a food choice were for business or social reasons, or if a food I had committed to eat had gone bad in the refrigerator. Because of her schedule, Diana could take my call only at 6:00 a.m. As I was rarely up before eight, I would get up at six, call her and tell her what I would eat for the day, eat my breakfast, and go back to sleep for a couple of hours before beginning my day.

I rebelled at this discipline. Deciding what I would eat and making a commitment was hard for me after having had no

---

*The experience I had with Diana and other sponsors and my experiences in different Twelve Step groups are not necessarily typical experiences. Sponsors and groups differ. A reader who is interested in attending a Twelve Step group for compulsive overeaters should attend several different meetings and choose the one that works best for him or her.

structure for years. I was so used to following my appetites and desires completely that I thought nothing of breaking my commitment to the food plan if I wanted to. The second morning after I began working with Diana, I wanted a diet soda as I sat working. But, I had agreed to drink only noncaffeinated soda. There were only caffeine drinks in my apartment, and I didn't want to take the time to go out to buy a noncaffeinated one. No big deal, I thought, as I grabbed a diet Dr. Pepper. At least I'm staying close to my food plan. I'm perfect in everything else and, after all, it isn't candy. I treated the program the way I had Weight Watchers. I was sure if I did my best and didn't eat any "bad" foods, Diana would understand. She didn't.

The next morning as I talked to Diana, I thought of omitting the fact I had had a caffeine soda, but something nudged at me until I told her. "I was working hard and didn't want to break to go out and get a soda without caffeine. Besides, I had to finish it since I wouldn't be having them anymore. . . . " My words trailed off into her dead silence.

"Heidi, this isn't a diet. You broke your commitment," she said. I felt indignant as she went on. "Recovery is about honesty and about going to any lengths to be freed of your compulsion. You committed to certain things, and if you don't have something that you need to stay on your food plan, you go out and get it."

Feeling a little injured — after all, I had done my best, and didn't that count for anything? — I went on to ask her if I could have sweetener on my cereal. "I need to have it because the wheat flakes are so plain," I told her.

"You don't *need* it, you *want* it," she responded. "God doesn't need the sweetener to keep you from compulsively overeating. You are relying on the sweetener to keep you abstinent. If you don't rely on God, you'll go back to relying on food."

That night I couldn't make myself eat the last few string beans. I'd committed to eat a cup. No less and no more. I had to eat them. I felt angry at Diana for controlling my food. Suddenly a memory of when I was five came to mind: Dad had pointed to my vegetables and admonished me to "stuff the junk down, Heidi." When I refused, he tugged me from my chair and took me to my bedroom, where he spanked me and left me for the evening. It had happened often. I tried to get past the rising anger at my father controlling my food to see Diana was only trying to help me with a choice *I* had made.

The pressure of my work made abstaining from compulsive overeating even more difficult. Food had become such an intrinsic part of my writing process that I panicked when I wasn't able to indulge in the reassuring habit of nibbling at cookies or eating several pieces of pie as I pondered how I would write the opening paragraph of an article. Before, as I had singlemindedly moved toward my writing goal, I ate whatever tasted good or promised myself a haven of food and television after I completed my work. Now, the sugar and caffeine withdrawal made working even harder. Headaches, depression, and shakiness plagued me.

A little over two weeks passed before I was able to see Diana in person again. In the days since she had become my sponsor, I had come to see how irregular my eating had been before. By letting someone else into my most secret corner, I also began to see the lengths to which I would go to protect my obsession. I saw how letting "little" commitments slide or shading the truth to suit my purpose was dishonest and destructive. But all this insight did nothing to change me or to make me more committed to the program.

⅔ ⅔ ⅔ ⅔ ⅔

When I took the train up to Connecticut two weeks after my first meeting there, I began a pivotal twenty-four hours in my recovery. I began to understand my distorted thought patterns and to see how closely my abuse paralleled that of alcoholics and drug addicts. I began to understand that I would have to surrender at a level deeper than I had conceived of before.

Somehow, the Connecticut meeting seemed even more threatening than the meetings in New York. I couldn't seem to rely on my indomitable perky exterior to keep people at bay, and it scared me. When I arrived at the meeting, the person who had picked me up at the station disappeared, and I moved almost stealthily to the back of the room, hoping to remain unnoticed. A woman intercepted me before I sat down. With an open look and a smile she introduced herself. I started my happy, bubbling words about my career, as I had with Diana the night I met her, but she didn't let it slide as Diana had. Instead, she looked me straight in the eye and said, "Cut the act. Tell me how you really feel."

I learned later that this is called *tough love,* and requires that people be totally honest and get right to their feelings. I felt a mixture of relief and fear in honestly facing these other people, people who were just like me — people who knew all my tricks. The look in these people's eyes wasn't unkind; in fact, it was a look that told me that they had experienced my darkest secrets and pain. It was as though they could see past whatever I was saying into how I really felt inside far better than I could. This room was a place where my wall of fat and charm didn't work to keep people from seeing my true self. No wonder I was uncomfortable.

The most scary thing about the evening was sitting there and realizing I was no different than those who were obsessive about alcohol or other drugs. This is what I have ahead of me, I thought, feeling consigned to a life of sackcloth and ashes as a "recovering addict." A life of deprivation, endless meetings in church basements, and requisite service in order to have God free me from my addiction to food. Will I ever again lead a normal life? I looked around the room at people who had been coming to this meeting every week for years. I found it unbearably depressing.

The other Heidi, the one of the sparkling career and exciting life of travel, seemed to be dying. None of it mattered if I was consumed with an addiction. I'm in a room full of people who use substances to retreat from life, I thought, as I saw a drunk man stagger in and sit down. That is reality. After he yelled a few times, interrupting the meeting, someone guided him into the hallway. With acute amazement I realized I was no different than him; I just didn't make a scene when I was numbed out on sugar. Yet, when I was controlled by food, I was just as disoriented and belligerent on the inside as he was on the outside.

After the meeting I stayed overnight at Diana's, and the next morning I sat on her bed, and we talked while she ironed some clothes. I felt as though I was being grilled by a parent as she asked how I felt these days — about food, but mostly about life. After an hour or so, she sat on the bed next to me. "When I first agreed to work with you, I did it because I was so excited for you. I like you and want you to recover," she said. "But we should have talked for a while first."

My heart was sinking. Was she going to drop me? Wasn't I good enough? Had I done something wrong? What? She went on to say that though I had tried to motivate myself to work the program, somewhere inside me I had figured that I could still beat the game. Food was still working for me: I was still getting something from it — escape, consolation, companionship — something. And I wasn't willing to go to any lengths to recover. I wasn't bad because of it, she said. It was just reality. Because I wasn't ready to surrender wholeheartedly to working the program, she said it wouldn't do any good for her to sponsor me. "When you are ready, you'll know it deep inside. And I'll be happy to work with you then," she said.

First I was angry, and then I defiantly decided that I would just get another sponsor — one who appreciated me. But, gradually, the truth of her words seeped in. I thought I was humble, grateful, and willing to bend to God's will, but I wasn't. There was a hard edge inside, a rebelliousness at accepting the need to see that my way wasn't working and at being grateful that there was another way. Looking back over the past two weeks, I had to admit I was angry that I was a compulsive overeater and angry that someone else was telling me what I could and couldn't eat. Diana said I wasn't wrong to feel that way, but I had to face my feelings and talk to God about them. Denying my anger and trying to motivate myself would only mean continuing to grudgingly comply with the program, which people in the program termed *white-knuckle abstinence*. It is what I had done the past two weeks, and eventually, it would lead me back to abusing food. I had to face the reality of the addiction in a deeper way in order to really change.

What could I do? I felt as though Diana were cutting off my lifeline. I sat quietly and listened, numbed by the thought of not having her as my security anymore. She told me that the founders of A.A. suggested that people who thought they could control their drinking try it. "Go out and try controlled eating, eating no sweets, and limiting your snacks," she said. "See how long it lasts."

No, I thought. Wasn't that what I had tried with Weight Watchers?

I didn't have to go back and binge, she said. What I had to do was face the truth. Going to program meetings and reading the Big Book would help, but in the end I would have to pray like crazy. I would have to ask my Higher Power to show me the truth about the damage my addiction had done in my life. Then, I had to feel the damage more deeply than I ever had in order to be willing to let go and learn how to cope another way. It would cause a deep, sharp pain, but the pain would diminish in time. And it would be better than the daily, dull, debilitating agony I endured now.

As I walked out of the house I was shaking. How did I go about *hitting bottom*, which is what everyone spoke of as a necessity for recovery? They said hitting bottom meant getting to the point where, in the deepest part of me, the food didn't work for me as an escape anymore. It meant reaching a place in my heart where I surrendered most profoundly to the truth that I am an addict. I was confused. I wanted to change more than anything, to get rid of this food obsession, yet my actions indicated that some part of me believed I could still control food. It showed that food still worked for me and that I did get my fix from food.

I was furious at Diana. Who was she to say I wasn't ready! I had done everything she asked of me. So, sometimes I forgot to take a snack with me as I had committed to. What was that? Then I slowly realized I had been treating the program like a diet club, something I could be detached from and work with in a logical, efficient way. But my gut-level terror told me this program wasn't something I could just observe while keeping my real emotions safely locked away.

I walked out of Grand Central Station as free as a bird to eat whatever I wanted. No sponsor. No binding food plan or even a set time to eat. It was terrifying. I missed the feeling of discipline I had felt on the food plan. I wanted it back. Yet

I felt delight, too, at the prospect of eating anything I wanted. Then the questions that used to rule my life only weeks earlier came back with shocking force: What do you desire to eat? What food do you most want now? I was curiously unexcited and felt a little frightened at re-entering the real world of food choices. I was shaky at the prospect of making decisions, remembering the lousy choices I had made for close to two decades. I was frightened of bingeing and of having the rest of my world unravel.

After that day with Diana, I felt as though I had to push the illness in me to the wall. The games I had been playing over the past two weeks were so deeply ingrained I hadn't even realized I was lying to myself. I thought I would do anything to recover, yet when pressed, I had found I wouldn't. I hadn't hit bottom. So I would try to make myself do it. Thus began a seven-month period where the healthy and logical side of me that understood I was a food addict methodically went about convincing the part of me that denied the truth. I was becoming aware, as many people in recovery discover, of a deeply angry child within me that wanted to deny my need to change.

I had thought this would be a time of joy and expectation, of hope in the knowledge that I needn't stay stuck in the misery of my compulsion. Instead I faced pain. At times I felt as though, in giving up the illusion that I controlled food, I were mourning someone who had died. The life I had led up to that point would never be the same again. That life — with its reliance on food and on controlling others — wasn't one I could sustain anymore. Now I saw it all, and it only caused me pain. I had always motivated myself to diet and had planned to apply that same will to make myself hit bottom. But hitting bottom couldn't happen unless I authentically faced what the illness had done to my life. I couldn't motivate myself to hit bottom. Hitting bottom didn't mean exerting more willpower; it meant surrendering.

I had to be willing to feel whatever pain came with facing the truth about myself. That, and only that, would create a desire for change. I could only pray for help to see what I needed to see, however painful. My heart had to truly surrender to letting go of food and the way I managed to get by in the past. It had to open to learning a new way of coping. For years now, the wisdom inside me had been pushed down as the food compulsion had taken over. Now, I had to listen quietly for that still, small voice of sanity, the voice from God. Somewhere early on I had chosen to use food, but I had long since lost my power of choice over food. I might as easily have used alcohol or other drugs. Food drugged me. I had to understand the seriousness of that.

As I carried on my solitary struggle, I told no one. I was so ashamed. I now saw myself as an addict. I couldn't even tell Greg. I was afraid I would seem crazy or overemotional when he called, so I put on a happy face as I had with others: I had never felt compelled to do that with Greg before. I began to experience the pain of the illness in a deeper way, and I was unable to explain it to Greg or anyone else.

I attended program meetings off and on over the next few months, but never consistently. When I did go I found solace in realizing that the people in the room knew my deepest secrets and that they were just like me. I couldn't fool them and didn't have to. I didn't feel compelled to keep up the image, chatting brightly and smiling all the time, that I still maintained for the outside world. They accepted me anyway, knowing the horror of what I did to myself and others. And it wasn't even so much my bingeing or weird food attitudes that caused me pain. It was my controlling, manipulative, deceitful behavior and attitudes that hurt me. That was what

I was so afraid of people finding out. I thought they would see the person I really was and be repulsed. I imagined that if people heard these thoughts, they would say, "No, that's not Heidi speaking. She's so sweet and considerate. She hasn't wronged anyone."

But the deepest part of me knew that the selfishness and fear the illness created in me were controlling and dishonest. Even though I thought I hadn't hurt anyone when I pulled out of dates or isolated myself, I saw now that I had. But I also began to hear people in my Twelve Step group say that I wasn't a bad person and that this was the way I had learned to cope and get what I needed. I remembered realizing the same thing with Maidi in Salzburg, where I saw my habits as separate from my core, and understood how true that perspective was.

Amazingly, it was during this time that I began to write for some of the big-name magazines that I had wanted to write for for years — *Working Woman*, *Bride's*, *Savvy*, and *McCall's*. Having begun to face what was wrong with my life, I realized I had rarely done my best before. Now I focused on simply doing the best I could with each article, and it paid off.

On the surface, my life was much the same as before or even better. But my view was shifting. My eyes were more honestly open to seeing the insidious pain that food and the coping mechanisms I developed had caused me. Not accepting what life was all about, I had tried to control everything around me. I suddenly saw how I had taken facts and arranged them according to my rigid ideas so that they fit my plan for what I wanted. Then, when people and events didn't conform to my plan, I became enraged.

Still, I clung tightly to my old ways of coping because they were so familiar. They allowed me to do all that was expected of me in the glamorous life I led, a life in which I felt so inadequate. The pressure got to me. The only way I seemed able to let off some steam was by reverting to what I already knew so well — food and my old habit of just getting by. For years I had precariously balanced my crazy life of writing, making a little money, and traveling all over the world. When I stepped in the unfamiliar territory of trying to live without using food as my crutch, I felt incapable of keeping up the bravado my life required. When I tried to face my addiction, my energies became totally absorbed by having to deal with feelings I had pushed down for so long.

Am I going to have to give up some of this glamorous life to focus on my recovery? I wondered one night as I paced the floor. It's either that or continue to kill myself little by little, all the while smiling as I travel around the world. I can't do both. I am like a child, a baby, and the only path is to reach out to God. I clearly cannot change on my own because I can't even see what my unhealthy attitudes are.

I finally opened myself up, praying to see the truth. Once I was really ready to listen, I got help: I woke every morning crying or depressed, as I was shown yet another way the illness had messed up my life. I began to see how it had affected people around me in ways I had just begun to understand. I would try to work, and instead be consumed with memories or thoughts of old, long-hidden pain.

The illusion that I was doing just fine as a fat, pretty woman, and that my life was manageable and working, began to fade fast. I could believe I was a successful travel writer, but how long would that last? I was getting assignments and often completed them well. But sometimes my down time with food and sleep caused me to turn in articles late and slack on quality too. I traveled to exotic places, yet found myself bingeing in my hotel room while others toured the area. I missed friendship, but saw how I often isolated myself from others. And how much longer could I put off my creditors and live overextended each month?

One day in late November I understood on a basic gut level that I was an addict. I had spent the afternoon in a movie theater downing popcorn and candy and then stopped at two stores for more food before going home. I'll just fix a nice dinner and get to work, I thought, rationalizing that I had just needed an afternoon off. Before I had even started cooking the chicken for dinner, I was obsessively thinking about what foods I *really* wanted and what I had in the apartment. The sweet stuff I had on hand included both cake and cookies, but what I really wanted was a scone. And all the salty and crunchy stuff I had were those pretzels. No, I want Doritos, I concluded and headed out to the corner store. That evening I finished off all the binge food in the house and fell exhausted into bed. I fell asleep, making a mental list of things that taste good, things that I had to get tomorrow.

Wide awake at 2:00 a.m., I had to have Häagen-Dazs vanilla ice cream and peanut butter. I have peanut butter and I can get the ice cream at that all-night store on the corner, I thought as I tucked my nightgown into the sweats I had pulled on. I headed for my coat. For a second, just one second, I paused as I pulled it on. An image of a disheveled drug addict obsessed with getting a fix flashed in my mind. I was momentarily paralyzed by the thought. But as quickly as the image had appeared, it was gone. No, maybe it was chocolate chip ice cream I wanted. I was out the door.

As dawn came, my mind was clearing. The sugar was fading and thoughts were pouring in. I was embarrassed as I thought about my "fantasy fix" the night before. Before going home for dinner, I had roamed the aisles of one store looking for something tantalizing and new. Not finding anything, I moved on to another store. I suddenly felt like a druggy seeking the ultimate high. The list of foods to try before I start the program just keeps getting bigger, I thought, as I heaved myself out of bed. There will never be enough. It will never end. At one time I had really believed there would be one last bite and then I would start my "diet." Now, I didn't. I wanted to say I'd go to any lengths to get rid of my compulsion, but I had to be able to say it honestly. It would be no good if I just complied; I had to really surrender. I keep thinking I've hit bottom, but have I? I wondered as panic filled me. Then something slipped over my brain, and I seemed to totally forget the night before as I focused on my upcoming trip to Vienna.

It wasn't until days later, when I was on another binge, that I knew I wouldn't be able to function much longer if I didn't beat this addiction. I hadn't been able to face the world that day and had simply turned off the phone, asking the answering service to pick up my calls. I spent most of the day weeping, thinking, and sleeping. I woke up a few minutes before the program meeting held at the YMCA, groaned, and rolled over to sleep some more. Some force, however, made me dress and pushed me out the door.

Stumbling in late to the meeting, I wore old sweat pants. My hair was uncombed, I was physically exhausted, my head hurt, and I felt an oppressive pain in my heart that wouldn't let up. I felt as if there was no way out of this pit, yet I knew there was. At that moment I felt like all the other fat people I had derided — but worse, I felt like an addict.

In the following days, I became densely apathetic about every thing and every person in my life. My senses dulled even to the excitement of travel. Greg had arranged to meet me in Vienna for a week at New Year's during my assignment there, but the thought hardly caused a flicker of interest inside me. I was still chasing highs in food, but even that rarely worked anymore. Still, at times it did its numbing job, and I kept seeking those moments. Food held out the promise that next time it would work, that a new kind of cake or enough Häagen-Dazs would give me a high.

Boredom and hopelessness pervaded my life. It was terrifying to think of the years ahead. I thought of myself in ten years, at age forty. The way the past years had so rapidly gone downhill, I knew the decline would only accelerate. But that wasn't what scared me most; what scared me most was the sameness. Ten years and nothing different. Me still sitting on the couch, obese, eating, watching television, and hiding out from the world, with no one in my life to be truly intimate with. The reality was that unless I changed, I would never have a husband and family: I could neither develop intimacy with a man nor function as a mother. Ahead I saw only many more days of intense struggle to merely survive.

ॐ ॐ ॐ ॐ ॐ

In Vienna with Greg, the noose tightened even more. We had been there only a few days when the subject of my weight came up. Our discussions brought me to a place I had never before been with a man. It was new for me to share this struggle with a man, to hear and understand his opinions, and to still maintain a relationship. I usually pulled away long before this point.

Greg mentioned a vegetarian food plan his mother and brother had lost weight on, believing in all sincerity that he could help me do what I most wanted to do — become more healthy and lose weight. He asked if I wanted to follow the plan with him for a couple of days, since he wasn't feeling great with all the heavy food we'd been eating. I listened to him, appalled at the idea of going through the next week without enjoying all the delicious foods of Vienna. It stupefied me that food was of such little importance to him that it didn't figure into his having fun on the trip. Food was my only source of excitement and joy most of the time these days, and Greg was actually suggesting that I give it up.

I agreed, of course, in order to please him, but I felt chained and enraged. When I ate something that wasn't on the plan, and Greg pointed it out, I felt both angry and naughty. It was as though my mother were monitoring my food once again. Within two days I resumed my double life — eating what he ate when we were together and then gobbling down creamy, starchy entrées at the business lunches I attended without Greg and following them up with rich Viennese desserts.

All the while I held tightly on to Greg's words in Vermont, that my being overweight didn't matter. I felt threatened now that he had actually expressed what he must have been thinking all along, that being overweight wasn't healthy or good. Every rational person thought the same way, but some part of my brain clung to the notion that somehow Greg saw me without noticing my weight. I held on to my fantasy belief that here was someone who thought I was perfect — because I thought I had to be perfect in order to be worthy of love.

My denial was punctured even further one morning over breakfast as we talked frankly about losing weight. "In the end it just comes down to doing it," Greg said. I looked at him, incredulous at how simple he made it sound. I knew better, especially with my recent realization of my food addiction. "It's about changing eating and exercise habits — self-discipline," he continued. My defenses went up instantly. Intended or not, behind his words I heard the assumption that I should lose weight and that I never should have become fat in the first place.

What could I say? Anything I might venture about the problems behind my weight would only sound like a defense or an excuse. In my own thinking, I had come to this place before, and my reasons for being overweight sounded hollow to me too. When Greg and I had spoken of the emotional side before, he'd been tolerant. I knew he understood it wasn't just about a diet, but I felt injured by the truth in his words — that it was going to take action, not just understanding, to lose weight. Perhaps his words struck too close to home. Isn't it about time you commit to recovery, Heidi? I thought, as I sat watching him benignly drink his orange juice. He had no idea of the impact his words had made. I had been messing around with dedicating myself to recovery for months. It was hard to take straight talk from him, but perhaps it was what I most needed at that moment.

Greg had pulled away one of my last props, and so I slid further downward. I was edgy the rest of the trip, responding angrily to him. As we settled in our seats on the flight home, I reached up to brush his cheek as I kidded him. When he pulled back, a terrible anger overtook me at the idea that he didn't want my touch. I didn't consider any other reason for his reaction. My anger was so strong that I had to get away from him. I spent most of the flight in a seat half a plane away. I was struck again by how damaging my illness had become. My fears and resentments were so deep that I realized I couldn't be around Greg anymore for very long or I would seriously hurt our relationship.

☙ ☙ ☙ ☙ ☙

In January an odd combination of physical ailments humbled me further, knocking out one more of my props. A week-long bout with the flu was followed by weeks in bed with a back injury. I had been determined to carry some shelves home and ended up straining my back so badly that I couldn't even sit up. I was impatient with the back pain, assuming I could push past it and get on with work. I couldn't. I slept many days, or lay in pain, forced to look at the reality of my life. I felt as though my body had joined my psyche in a battle to force me to surrender and change. My body's battle seemed to echo that of my heart, the healthy part of me that kept punching away at my denial of my illness.

It wasn't until the last week of January when Greg came to town on business that I was even walking again. I hadn't seen him since Vienna. I couldn't wait until he was gone so I could begin working on my recovery program. He was only a distraction from my mission now. I was determined that he not know how bad things had been for me emotionally. I was also terrified to face him now that I was bingeing most days. I couldn't let him in too close — partly because what I was going through was so intensely personal, and partly because I didn't want him to know the ugly details. I said to myself that I wanted him to have good memories of us, but it was more that I wanted him to have a good image of me. These days I felt so crazy I was sure I would ruin our time together. I was glad he was staying at a hotel instead of with me, as he often did. I never could have hidden the reality of my life from him then.

I despised the lie I was presenting to Greg, but knew no other way. One night toward the end of his visit, I had him over for a healthy, nutritious dinner. All week I had led him to believe I had been abstinent when actually I was bingeing. That night I sat there and lied to his face, telling him I was working my Twelve Step program. We had always been so honest with each other and now I was deceitful, and I felt horrible. After he left, I binged again.

The next day I turned on the answering service and didn't shower or dress until 6:00 p.m. Greg was still in town and had said he might come over later in the evening, but I had to get out of the apartment. By 8:30, I was weeping silently in the park on my corner. How much more could I take of this pain inside? My life on the outside didn't seem much different than it had been a year ago, but I saw it differently. I saw the manipulating and desire to control other people, the dishonesty in showing others only what I wanted them to see. I felt afraid of what others thought of me and of my feelings of loneliness, uselessness, and despair. I knew I didn't have it in me to overcome these obstacles. I needed God as I never had and felt somehow that God was there. But where? Why didn't He give me my "bottom" now? How much more pain would it take? In a moment of raw agony, I looked up to see Greg bouncing around the corner singing along with his Walkman.

I was so shocked I barely mumbled hello and then turned away. It never occurred to me he would show up as I sat in the park. I didn't understand then how important it was that he arrived in the midst of my suffering. His unexpected appearance was perhaps the only way I would have let a friend into the heart of my pain, opening the door on the isolation and shame of my addiction. My first instinct, however, was to protect my "together" image. We started walking back toward my apartment. He asked what was wrong.

Greg had caught me with my defenses down. I didn't have the brainpower to come up with my usual glib answers. I couldn't think; I couldn't respond. I wondered how far I could let him in. I didn't think I had the option of simply telling him what I felt and taking my chances. My misery would be too much for anyone to listen to, and the raw wound was too ugly for other eyes to see. He asked again what was wrong, and I answered, "What do you mean?"

He simply said, "I'm not buying that! Do you think I'm blind?"

I felt claustrophobic at the thought of talking in my apartment, so I asked if we could walk the other way. We ended up in a coffee shop nearby, and in fits and starts I told him about my addiction to food and how I had glossed over it before, representing the Twelve Step program as a diet club or only a support group. I explained it was like alcoholism, that I hadn't been able to hit bottom, and that now I was terrified for my life. He simply took my hand and listened.

The next day as he left for the airport, he hugged me warmly. Without saying a word about our conversation, I knew he understood and was still there for me. In the next days, I felt as though so much was methodically clicking into place. Avenues of escape were being closed as the realities of my illness relentlessly faced me. And I was glad for it. Even as another seemingly bad thing happened in my life, I knew it would deepen my surrender and bring about eventual relief. I felt that God was answering my prayers, helping me finally reach a place from which I could move toward a peace I had never known in my life. There was now an acceptance in me that hadn't existed a few weeks earlier. I felt a patience and willingness to see what I needed to see, even as I binged. I couldn't control the bingeing, and I knew each time as I watched myself gorge again, that my path of change — the moment when I couldn't do it anymore — was finally coming. I wasn't rushing to commit to recovery in a moment of horror. Instead, I was moving to the moment of commitment through experiencing a deep, constant pain that wouldn't subside. The pain stayed with me most days now, intensifying as I looked at the reasons for it in my life.

❧ ❧ ❧ ❧ ❧

In late February I decided to try a liquid protein diet, a supervised program at Rockefeller University that would get me started on weight loss. I went to program meetings occasionally, but I thought I would just lose some weight first and then start my recovery. Most of my heart believed that I was a compulsive overeater and that I was going to have to permanently change. But some corner still wanted to try dealing with my illness my way — one more time. So here I was trying something I swore I would never bother with. I had always prided myself on never taking silly, drastic measures. And now I was drinking four packets of Carnation Instant Breakfast a day, taking an assortment of vitamins, and brushing three times a day to exercise my gums. Two weeks later, and twelve pounds lighter, I realized the diet had made me more obsessed with food than ever.

I was completely out of control with food and rage. The obsession was so much more evident to me, yet I had less control than ever. I reached for whatever foods I thought would satisfy me and seemed incapable of stopping myself. And worse, I couldn't turn off my conscious mind now. I was totally aware of my uncontrollable behavior as I reached like an addict for my substance. I was furious with everyone in my life. Mostly, I was angry at God for giving me this illness, for not letting me eat like other people.

I felt like a lunatic for a couple of weeks. I was barely civil to friends and felt as if I should just keep away from people or I would damage all my friendships and, worse, tarnish my image. The pressure built up in me at having to act normal and run my career at full tilt while feeling dead inside. Through it all was a sadness that perhaps I had hit bottom a few weeks before and, grabbing at an easier way, had blown it by trying the liquid protein diet instead of seeking recovery through the Twelve Steps. Some part of me had really believed I could just go on that diet and lose weight. But if I believed that, then I hadn't really hit bottom.

Until the last few days of March, another part of me believed that what I had to do was "simply" take myself in hand and motivate myself to change. Self-control was all I needed. Then, a series of days created a hopelessness that I had never known before, as all-out bingeing and self-indulgent depression gripped me. I was appalled at the amount of food I was able to eat. Usually I stopped because I got so full it hurt, but now I stuffed myself like never before, until I was physically sick. I knew what I was doing, but knowing wasn't enough to make me stop. My excuses were insanely trivial and so familiar: I'll start tomorrow and finish the goodies in the house first; my finances are depressing me; I'm under so much pressure in my career. I watched my thought process, but I was powerless to stop it.

It was the third day I had spent frantically trying to deny my emotions by covering them with eating pudding, ice cream, and cake, going to movies, or sleeping. . . . As I came home from the movies that day, I picked up a dozen Austrian pastries; they encompassed all my warm, carefree memories of being a student in Salzburg. The phone was ringing as I walked through the door. It was Greg. He sounded worried and said he had called off and on all afternoon because he knew one of my articles had been canceled and that money was tight.

"Listen, could we talk later? I just walked in the door," I said, feeling shaky and eager to eat and wanting to get off the phone.

By the time he called back an hour later, I had consumed most of the pastries and was feeling just fine. Frankly, I couldn't have cared less whether he called back at all. An invisible pillow of insulation rested between us as I tried to follow the threads of his conversation. "Gee, this must really be upsetting you," Greg said, alarmed at my brief, uncommunicative responses. "It's going to be alright. There will be other assignments. Do you need some money?" he went on, trying to help me.

I just wanted to finish the rest of my food and go to bed. I felt as if everything was far off and didn't make much sense or matter. I was drugged. He seemed to think I was upset. What a laugh. Instead, I was as numb as I had ever been in my life, unconcerned with him and barely able to keep up a conversation. Finally, we said good-bye, and I flopped into bed.

As I drifted off to sleep, an image appeared in my mind that had come up repeatedly in recent months. I was waxing a kitchen floor and had somehow waxed myself into a corner near the back door. There I stood, precariously balancing on the last square. Outside was an extraordinarily beautiful, sunny garden, but I stood stubbornly in my corner, screaming at anyone who tried to help me make the jump outdoors. As my corner kept shrinking, I knew the jump was inevitable, and it terrified me. The only thing standing between me and the beauty I saw was my reluctance to surrender and my unwillingness to venture into the unknown.

The next morning was Friday. I had a sugar hangover and was on my knees as I had been so many times in recent months, praying to finally reach a place in my heart where I was willing to change and let go of food. Screaming and pounding on the floor, I was angry at myself for not being able to get motivated and angry at God for not helping me hit bottom. When I had prayed in the past I had asked God to help me, but a corner of me had always held back. I hadn't been totally willing to give up the ways I had been using food to cope and to try another way. And until I was, God couldn't lift the obsession. But that morning as I had awakened, I felt with *all* my heart that I couldn't go on as I had been and that I was willing to completely change my orientation on life. And now, as the anger subsided, I prayed for God to lift my obsession and to help me make it through the day by turning to God instead of food. With a tearful laugh, I realized that finally I really meant it.

That morning I made out a healthy food plan for the day and followed it until the evening, when I binged on popcorn, and bananas with peanut butter. Ironically, bingeing didn't change me from my path, but reinforced my feeling that I wanted to rely on God to make me well. I hadn't turned to my classic binge foods, though I was overeating. My stomach ached with fullness.

On Saturday, I spent a strange day of bingeing intermittently. Then, even though I intended to binge that evening, something inside propelled me to a friend's going-away party instead. That night I went to bed feeling that I had made at least some choices that had taken me away from food.

Sunday was a day full of a kind of tender, loving care and nurturing that I had never felt from a human source. I felt again the determination to be abstinent. But more than that, I wanted to be where God would have me be and to do the things I needed to do to take care of myself and recover. I knew I didn't have control and that, when the temptation arose, I would ask God to help me. It was the second day of a weekend conference at my church, so I took my food with me and planned to lunch with friends between sessions of the conference. At lunch they ordered Chinese food, and I thought of changing my plans or eating alone and then realized I needn't do either. I would just bring my tuna and salad with me. My recovery was the most important thing in my life that day. It meant keeping the commitment I had made to myself and God that morning, but it didn't mean not being with people. I felt so different than I had a few months earlier when I would have resented following my food plan with friends. I no longer feared or resented doing what I had to in order to recover.

All that day I found myself seeking to know God's will when something came up. When I felt tense because of my expectations and fears about work or friends, I said a prayer, asking

God to guide me and to let me do His will in the situation. A calmness spread through me. I felt frightened to speak of the precious and sacred change that had occurred in my heart, wondering if it would evaporate if I did. Toward the end of the afternoon conference session, in the large hall crowded with people, I could feel that some key of surrender had turned slowly within me over the past couple of days. Slipping out of the room, I went into the bathroom for a moment alone. There I kneeled, wept, and prayed in gratitude for the change that had been made in my desires and perspective. My heart lifted and sang. When I was finally completely willing, God came with overwhelming force to help me.

CHAPTER SEVEN

Detoxing Body and Soul

Spring 1987 — Winter 1988

I walked into a program meeting the day after my surrender looking for a sponsor. The people I had seen who were recovering — who didn't seem to be fighting food or the world anymore — had thoroughly worked the Steps. So I knew that's what I had to do to recover too. That meant finding someone who had done it and asking that person to guide me through the Steps. I had also heard that it was wise to choose a sponsor whom you admired and aspired to be like. With that in mind, a few weeks earlier I had asked a woman who had lost 120 pounds if she would sponsor me, only to find out that she was already sponsoring several recovering compulsive overeaters.

Tonight, I was looking for that statuesque blonde actress I had seen before in meetings. That's what I want to be like, I thought. When she didn't show up for the meeting, I sat down next to Renee, feeling a little deflated. As I greeted her, a light bulb went off in my head. Renee hadn't lost 120 pounds, and she wasn't my dashing picture of recovery, but she possessed the qualities I was after. She had a gentle serenity and a sane attitude toward food. She had solidly worked the Steps and knew how to help me do the same.

When I asked her to sponsor me, she immediately gave me an assignment to write a complete review of my history of compulsive overeating, including all the ways I had tried to control food and my weight. This was the first of several assignments that Renee gave me to take me through the first three Steps, all of which are intended to help compulsive overeaters look at the damage food abuse has done to their lives and reach a place where they can rely on a Higher Power to help them recover.

Only three days later I headed out on the first test of my commitment to the program, a press trip to a Florida resort. It was the first time I would be traveling for my career while trying to be abstinent. I was terrified. Excuses to avoid starting a diet had long been a way of life for me. I groaned to recall how recovering compulsive overeaters had said in program meetings that they put off vacations so they could stay abstinent, not wanting to be tempted with luscious foods. Was I crazy to go?

Calling the trip organizer ahead of time to find out what we would be eating so I could commit to it, I recalled Renee's words that morning. "You can't just step out of life until you recover. How many times did you say you would do that with a diet? This isn't a diet. If you rely on God to lift the obsession to binge, He will help you do what you have to in order to stay abstinent." The plausible-sounding excuses I had made only weeks before to delay abstinence now seemed silly. Renee was right. I couldn't step out of life to recover. I had to do it here and now, every day of my life.

The first night in Florida I was heady with the excitement of keeping my commitment. After checking in to a hotel, I met the press group by the pool for a buffet dinner. These trips were usually an excuse for everyone to overindulge, and the buffet spread before me would normally have induced a feeding frenzy in me. But the first hint of feeling deprived was quickly replaced by gratitude that I wasn't driven to stuff everything in sight in my mouth. Instead, I concentrated on finding the chicken, bread, salad, and apple the trip organizer had said would be there; these things would fit into my food plan.

As the others settled themselves at tables near the pool, I unobtrusively weighed and measured my food. Then, I sat with some of the members of the British press who were there to cover the same international croquet match I would be writing about. For the first time in my life, eating seemed secondary to getting to know people. On the surface, the scene was one I had experienced dozens of times before, but I listened now with heightened senses. I felt more alive, as though a soft, spongy wall had been removed so I could interact with others more fully. Leaning back in my chair to cut my apple for dessert, I realized I was not preoccupied with food that evening. I had no desire to leave early so I could binge in the privacy of my room. Instead I looked forward to talking with the people around me — that had become my source of enjoyment.

When I returned to my room a couple of hours later, I found three mints on my pillow. Picking them up, I glanced over at the fruit and cheese basket left by the management. Although I could have fruit and cheese on my food plan, I was sure to be served the portions I needed at meals, so it seemed silly to have the basket sit there. And I'll never need these mints, I thought with a laugh, as I looked down at the candy in my hands. No point in having them around to tempt the obsession.

Gathering the basket and candy, I loaded down a maid passing by in the hall. As I lay in bed after praying that night, I realized what a miracle it was to be going to bed feeling clean about what I had eaten that day, clean and at peace. I hadn't had to fight with myself over food today. Away from the public eye, I would normally have been eating, or at the very least, thinking obsessively about food and wishing I could binge to make myself numb. But now, I felt settled inside and saw that I was starting to turn away from destructive food habits and toward God. God had blessed me each day that week with sane eating.

But my new attitude toward food was only part of the change, I realized, as I thought back on the evening. I had felt more open toward those around me, less defensive and fearful of what they thought, more interested in their needs, and less concerned about getting something from them.

The next night wasn't so euphoric. At 10:30 p.m., I was sitting alone in my hotel room, having left a jovial group of journalists partying in the disco. I was in a state — physically and emotionally — that I had been in scores of times before at various resorts throughout the world. As I took off my shoes and began to undress, I puzzled over what had just happened inside me; I was facing a dilemma that I had faced as a fat woman before, and once again I was unsure if I was over-reacting.

Dinner was never a problem for me on these trips. I usually had some man or other seated next to me, chatting and making me feel good. But, inevitably, a chance comment or action punctured my fragile self-confidence. That night Ross, a savvy, good-looking writer for the British magazine *Harper's & Queen* sat with me at dinner. We talked about his work and mine, about New York and London. Then, as we were finishing dessert and coffee, he began talking to Lilly, the petite beauty who headed the resort's public relations department. As the meal ended I heard him say, "You look so beautiful in pink," touching her arm and helping her up. It was as though I wasn't there. As it was happening, I felt that somehow I had been negated as a woman because of my weight.

Sitting in my room, I wondered why the comment had pierced me so, coming as it did from a man I had just met. But a familiar suffocating sadness had descended over me at his words, and I slid uncontrollably from sparkling conversationalist to introspective soul-searcher. I was suddenly more guarded and less confident. The group moved on to the disco, but I couldn't capture the lightness I had felt earlier. I had lost my mask of confidence and had plunged into self-hate. I felt silly in my cocktail dress. I knew no one would want to dance with me. I mumbled an excuse that I was tired and headed to my room. Without the numbness sugar provided, my pain was acute. But food isn't an option, I thought with resignation. I curled up in bed alone with the pain, unsure of what else to do.

๛ ๛ ๛ ๛ ๛

I had been so high with the newness of beginning to work the Steps to recovery and with the trip, that it was a few days after my return to New York before caffeine and sugar withdrawal hit me. When it hit, it hit hard. I arrived from Florida Sunday night, and by Monday morning, as I tried to work, I was plagued with a headache, depression, and the shakes.

For most of my thirty years, much of the food I had eaten had been refined sugars and carbohydrates. Now my diet was balanced with protein, fruit, vegetables, and complex carbohydrates — virtually no sugar, except in fruit. Suddenly, I was going through the process of withdrawal from what was for me an addictive substance.

I began to feel hunger for the first time. It came sporadically at first, as though my body wasn't quite sure what was going on. Within a few weeks, I began to feel normal hunger pangs after several hours of not eating. Hunger, which I had rarely experienced before because I had grazed on food, began to be a normal sensation, alerting me that it was time to eat.

One morning two weeks into abstinence, I sat at my computer, paralyzed with fear, wondering how I would ever endure the initial withdrawal — both physically and psychologically. Unencumbered by a sugar fog, my feelings were alive and on a rampage inside me. Just keep breathing, I thought, and it will get easier. My moods fluctuated now for little or no reason. The lethargy and depression I thought would somehow miraculously be gone when I was abstinent grew stronger. Overwhelming feelings would suddenly descend on me, leaving me staring into space, not knowing what to do.

But I have to work today. I groaned inwardly at how all my energy over the past two weeks had been consumed by keeping my commitment to eating what I told Renee I would, and doing the writing assignments for the Steps. I wasn't sure how to work without my crutch. I had always snacked while I wrote, wandering into the kitchen for some cookies between phone interviews and the like. Now I still had to earn money, but I didn't want to do it as I had before, eating compulsively throughout the day.

A couple of weeks later, I realized that not only did my body have to go through withdrawal from my past habits, my mind did too. I woke up depressed, but couldn't put my finger on why. Then, I stopped myself, thinking, No, that isn't how I feel anymore. I have hope. It was as though the depression I had wakened with for the past couple of years had become a habit, one born of hopelessness at ever finding an answer to my weight problem. Rolling over in bed to look out the window at a clear blue sky, I remembered that I had experienced almost three weeks of clean abstinence. A miracle, I thought, and smiled. A gift from God. I feel positive and protected from food. I am beginning to fix my life.

That afternoon I took my Third Step. First, I knelt alone in my apartment and committed to God that I would try life His way, then later I read a special prayer with my sponsor in a small chapel before the program meeting. At first I had feared that turning my life and my will over to God would mean giving up some part of me, or that I could never make another mistake. But walking home that night I felt a gentleness inside and an acceptance of this tiny step that I had taken to learn a new way of coping with life, a way that wasn't devastating to my soul.

The first of many times I would weigh and measure my food in one of New York's best restaurants occurred a week later. This tested my commitment and my promise of rigorous honesty, as well as slicing down my ego a bit. As I walked into the 21 Club and took the elevator to a private dining room for a press luncheon, I felt in my coat pocket for my scale and measuring cup. They were there, and they stayed in the pocket as I hung up my coat and joined the group enjoying pre-lunch cocktails and appetizers. A few minutes later, over polite conversation with the host of the luncheon, I plucked a couple of shrimp off a plate offered me. This is okay, I thought. I committed to eat six ounces of protein for lunch, so I could have some shrimp and use the remaining ounces for the veal at lunch. Two shrimp, I thought. They probably total an ounce.

But something stopped me as I started to pop them in my mouth. I had committed to weigh and measure everything I ate now, to learn normal portion sizes. Putting the shrimp in a napkin, I excused myself and headed down the hall to the coat closet.

"May I help you?" the maître d' proprietarily sniffed as I walked past him.

"No, thank you," I said as I sailed by. Pulling out the scale, I placed it on an antique table near the ladies' room and carefully weighed the shrimp. Ignoring the penetrating eyes of the maître d' staring at me from across the hall, I noted that indeed the shrimp weighed one ounce. Placing the shrimp in my napkin, I put the scale back in my coat, grinned at the maître d', and without a word of explanation, headed back to the cocktail party.

As I left the 21 Club, having used the scale at the table to weigh and measure all I ate, I marveled at my willingness to go to any lengths to be rid of my obsession. My growing commitment to recovery wasn't anything I could really touch or see, yet it was so tangible inside. I realized that my new attitudes toward food and life seemed every bit as miraculous to me as the miracle of the blind man in the Bible suddenly seeing. Something had turned around in my heart, and my desires had changed. I didn't want to binge. Even more, I really wanted to give up the painful attitudes of fear and resentment that were at the base of my addiction.

How is it possible for me to actually have my desires change, to want to try it God's way instead of my own? I wondered as I walked down Fifth Avenue on my way home. A few weeks ago, the addict in me would have asked, What do I get from doing God's will, and why would I want to let go of control? I shuddered, remembering the suffocating hopelessness I had felt so recently. My way didn't work. God's way had so far. I felt settled and happy.

୫ ୫ ୫ ୫ ୫

The first of May, I began my Fourth Step inventory. The inventory was a fact-facing mission where I reviewed what caused my past problems and admitted the complete truth to myself. For the next several weeks, most of my free time focused around doing my Fourth Step work, which meant writing out in detail my character defects, fears, past resentments, and attitude problems in various relationships.

Painful as it was to review past anxieties and face my defects, I had a sense of purpose and felt secure and cozy during the time I was working on the Fourth Step. Going through my journal one night to find the resentments I needed to list, I was sickened to encounter a painful moment that I had experienced with a friend in college. What a relief it will be to let that go, I thought. It made me happy to think that when I finished, I wouldn't have such a dirty feeling about the past. Closing my journal, I wished I were going faster. It's been only a few weeks, Heidi, I reminded myself. Recovery is a process that happens tiny step by tiny step.

Ironically, even as my food problem was being lifted, I could see more clearly the knee-jerk reactions that had made my emotions so uncontrollable. Just a few hours earlier when I called Greg, he had been short with me. I quickly hung up and began my typical downward spiral into depression. What have I done? What's wrong with our relationship? I worried. Then suddenly my thoughts shifted. Maybe, just maybe, he's having a rough day, Heidi. What a novel idea. I laughed out loud. Something is wrong with him that has absolutely nothing to do with me or our relationship. I'm in kindergarten and this relationship business is graduate school level, I thought as I turned back to my Fourth Step work. My priority has got to be recovery. I'll figure the rest out later.

I found myself using the other Steps I was learning in the program to work through the fear and anger that I faced in my daily life. Using the daily Tenth Step inventory, I was able to analyze what was causing me anxiety in a situation and what part I played in it. Often the feelings were lifted as I concluded the inventory with a prayer. One day at *Successful Meetings*, I stuck my head in Susan's office to say hello and get an assignment she had promised to give me for an upcoming issue of the magazine. Instead of giving the assignment, she said, "Melissa said you might be too busy with other article assignments for this particular issue, Heidi."

Trying to contain the fury that leapt to my throat, I smiled. What business was it of Melissa's what assignments I get? I thought, terrified that I wouldn't get the assignment and the money I counted on making from it. Recognizing that my emotions were raging, I told Susan I'd get back to her in a minute and went to sit at my desk.

I stepped back from the situation, went through my feelings step by step as my sponsor had taught me, and prayed for God to show me what to do. First, what does it affect in you, Heidi? Why do you feel so threatened? There was definitely fear that Susan wasn't giving me the assignment because she didn't like my work. With that came the fear that she wasn't going to give me any more assignments. It affects my finances because I need to earn all the money I can to pay off debts. And it affects my pride because I want what I want, and how dare she not give it to me, I thought with a laugh. I realized that I had caught myself thinking like a child in the middle of a tantrum.

Suddenly, I could see where I was wrong in the situation. Melissa, Susan's supervisor, shouldn't have to call a halt to my overbooking my time. That should have come from my own internal regulator. Obviously, Susan had been afraid to tell me, and when she had relayed Melissa's message, I had pulled back all my warmth from Susan. I was shocked to see how controlling I had been with Susan. Sweet Heidi who never gets angry, who is never rude; she's all smiles and kindness until she doesn't get what she wants. Then, although I didn't show outright anger, I withdrew my friendship.

As my last step in the inventory, I considered corrective measures. Making an extra effort to joke with Susan, I was also frank with her in conceding that Melissa was probably right about my taking on too much. Susan said she'd be happy to assign me an article for the next issue. Somewhere along the way, my resentment toward Melissa vanished. As I headed home, I was amazed at how quickly I had felt settled. Before, I would have denied the anger and fear, and it would have stayed inside me. I would have felt insecure because I would have believed that Melissa didn't think I was good enough as a writer. And I would have become wary of Susan because I would have thought she didn't like me. It felt so wonderful to begin to deal with reality.

ঙ ঙ ঙ ঙ ঙ

As my body and mind cleared, I found I didn't need as much sleep as I had, and I actually had the desire to exercise daily. One morning in late May I was riding a stationary bicycle at the YMCA when I looked up at the clock. It read 6:30. Looking in the mirror, I abruptly stopped my pedaling as a grin spread across my face. This sure isn't the Heidi I know, I thought with joy. I've become a woman who is up early, wants to work out, and feels comfortable at the Y. Even as I thought it, I knew it was the result of a discipline from a Power higher than myself.

Pedaling on, I thought about how all the parts of my day seemed more relaxed now. I could work the whole day on various projects without tension and frustration, without feeling pressure to accomplish, without fear of being late with articles. Praying to be shown what my priorities should be, I was able to relax and trust that I would get help as I methodically worked through my daily list. Without all the fear of what editors would or wouldn't think about me, I became much more productive. I felt the sheer delight of making a date with friends and not pulling out at the last minute to succumb to the compulsion to hide out with my food. It wasn't easy, and at moments I longed for the security of solitude, but I prayed to be able to continue trying this new way of being with people.

My recovering lifestyle was put to a test for two weeks in June when I flew to Hawaii for *McCall's* magazine. Arriving at the Mauna Kea Beach Hotel on the Big Island of Hawaii was like coming home. I had been to the hotel before, and this time I was in the beach wing and had a palm-fringed view of the surf. As I unpacked, I pondered what I would do that afternoon before meeting the resident manager for dinner. Instinctively, I reached for the room-service menu, my mouth watering as my eyes washed across all the food choices. Before, I would have ordered room service and sat on the balcony with a big lunch and then slept all afternoon. Putting the menu down, I wondered what else to do. I could do some writing on my Fourth Step or read. Looking out the window, I fleetingly thought of swimming or snorkeling.

Then I looked at the bed — sleep. Not knowing what else to do, I turned off my brain and dove into the pillows for a nap. Waking a couple of hours later, I felt lethargic and, in a faint way, as if I had binged. I hadn't binged, but I'd reverted to the pattern of escaping that I'd used on past trips. That isn't me anymore, I thought.

The next morning, determined to be a new, recovering Heidi, I dressed in a swimsuit and sweatpants and headed down to the health club to ride the stationary bike. After working up a sweat, I went to the beach for a swim in the tranquil lagoon. Few people were on the beach, and I felt uninhibited as I pulled off my sweats and waded into the warm, shimmering water. How wonderful to feel my body work, I thought, my muscles aching a bit as I swam out to a float. I'd lost almost forty pounds in the past three months, and my body felt lighter. Soaking in the morning sun, I watched colorful tiny fish flickering above the sand ripples twenty feet below in the clear water.

For the next few days, I vacillated between times when I stayed in touch with myself, exercising and working on my

Fourth Step, and hours when I unconsciously turned off inside, as if I were on vacation from my program of recovery. The day after my first swim, I went swimming early again, read for a while on the beach, and then found myself ordering lunch to eat on the balcony. Staring now at the french fries the waiter had brought with my hamburger, I tried to figure out how I could have some. Well, I can have potatoes on my food plan, and I can have oil. So if I combine the two I can have french fries, I rationalized. I'll have those instead of the hamburger bun. A nagging doubt reminded me I should make no food changes until I talked with my sponsor, but I shoved the doubt aside and picked up a french fry. Because I'm committing my food plan on a postcard to Renee, I won't have to deal with the consequences until I get back, I thought defiantly. Finishing my lunch, I napped.

When I arrived at the Stouffer Wailea Beach Resort on Maui the next day, there was a message from the resort's public relations manager that she wanted to take me to dinner. I was enraged. I had secretly been looking forward to being alone with my dinner and was jealously guarding my lazy alone hours. "Wait," I said in midthought. Something was really off if I wanted to isolate myself from others. That was a behavior associated with the illness. I thought back on the past few days when I had been alone; it hadn't helped my depression. I couldn't escape so easily into food and fantasy now — I missed people. Isolating myself didn't work for me anymore, especially without the drug of food, but I didn't know how to be with people. Sometimes it was too hard. Recalling how offhandedly I had shifted my food plan to include french fries, I was shaken to realize how that first compulsive bite could have led to a full-blown binge.

Before I went to dinner, I called my sponsor. "Get to a meeting," she said. "But first, trace the feeling of being off track to where it started. What fears and resentments have you been denying?"

I sat down and wrote, discovering within me an angry, petulant child who didn't want to face work and reality. Looking down at the rash on my arms from the sun, I realized I was irrationally furious that I couldn't stay out in the sun all day until I got a golden tan. I was afraid I wouldn't look good without a tan when Greg joined me in a few days for the second week of my stay. More anger — that I can't eat what I want, that I have to meet the obligations of work and spend so much time with people from the resorts where I stayed, that I can't isolate myself. All of this was part of the illness. I'd been blustering around, ignoring the sane route, and look where it got me! I had started out by ignoring my daily program work — not reading the Big Book, not praying, and not working on the Fourth Step — and within a few days I was pondering an escape back into food.

As I took the elevator down to the restaurant to meet the public relations manager, I felt humbled at seeing how quickly the illness could devastate me again. My sponsor had said I must redouble my efforts on vacation, because it's natural to also want a vacation from the program. But I wasn't prepared for this wall. My willingness to work had come so easily once I had finally hit bottom. Then suddenly I was slapped with these childish attitudes and the defects I thought I had been so good about changing. Overnight, I'd returned to the habits of napping, reading for escape, and focusing on food. I felt angry at almost everything that wasn't going just my way.

The next morning, I flew to the island of Molokai for the day, returning to Maui that evening in time to meet Greg's flight from the mainland. After a couple of near-perfect days at the Hotel Hana Maui on the far side of the island, we flew on to Kauai, where several experiences brought me face to face with my body — as it was and as it was becoming. Arriving at the Coco Palms Resort, I was at first forlorn when the hotel management gave Greg and me separate rooms. Then I realized that I had been trying to create a romantic fantasy again. That night, as I reviewed my day and did my Step work before going to bed, I was glad for the cushion of privacy having my own room gave me. The past week had fortified my desire to put my recovery first, and in my room I really wanted to work on it without having Greg around.

A few days later, Kenai Helicopter arranged a complimentary flight for Greg and me along the famous Na Pali Coast and into the center of a volcano. When we walked into the office that morning, the pilot asked each of us our weight so he could better balance the chopper for its close-flying run through the volcano and over cliffs. My heart sank. I weighed 290, but I couldn't say it out loud. Not with Greg there. Frantically I tried to figure out how much lower I could say my weight was. Without even thinking I might be putting the lives of the crew and other passengers in danger by throwing off the chopper's balance, I said 240 pounds.

I climbed nervously into the helicopter. A precocious eight-year-old boy, placed in the seat between Greg and me for balance, began whining about not being by the window. He asked why he couldn't be on the outside. He quieted only a bit when the pilot explained that the helicopter required equal weight along both sides. Blushing intensely and despising the child, I turned to look out the window as we rose over the lush scenery. Tears stung my eyes. I was constantly aware that I weighed more than Greg. It was horrible enough for me to face it without having it thrown in his face too. At first I hardly noticed the extraordinary view, but when we flew into the mossy oasis of the volcano I caught my breath and forgot myself.

Spending time with Greg on the beach should have been wonderful, but it was mostly agonizing. I sat there like a blob, making the excuse that I couldn't go in the water because I'd get burned and the rash would flair up again. But, of course, it was really that I couldn't let him see me in my swimsuit without the *pareo*, a South-Seas-style wrap skirt that somewhat covered my thighs. Again, I felt cornered by my weight. More than anything, I wanted to be out there playing and laughing in the waves with Greg, but instead I was locked into my square of beach.

Later, at the pool, a woman with a perfect body sat next to us. I tried to concentrate on what Greg was saying about our management book, but my heart wasn't in it.

"Heidi, what's on your mind?" he asked as I stared off into the palm trees above. At some point I wanted to share these feelings, but at that moment I felt too vulnerable to tell him about being insecure about my sexuality and self-esteem.

Looking straight ahead, sunglasses in place, I tried to explain. "Even though I've lost some weight, I have a long way to go," I said tentatively, glancing over at him to see how he was reacting. "I feel so inhibited now by the way I look, and I feel frustrated by it."

He looked at me and smiled warmly. "Heidi. No one has a timetable. No one's watching. It takes time. I really admire your determination in doing this," he said and then added with a chuckle, "I've seen how faithfully you weigh and measure all your food, even in restaurants. That's commitment!"

A few days later we were sitting on the beach at Waikiki in the late afternoon when I looked up and saw an enormous woman in a two-piece swimsuit talking unself-consciously to friends — directly in our line of vision. My insides twisted as I watched Greg watch her, then turn and look at me. As he continued talking lazily about what we planned to do in the afternoon, my mind raced. Dare I ask him what he's thinking?

No. I better think of something to say to separate me from her in his mind. Change the topic. Say something that will get his attention off her. Talk about the book or his work. No. No. Just run screaming down the beach away from him, away from her, away from my horrible feeling that he thinks I'm just like her and is completely repulsed.

"So, Heidi, what do you want to do? Shopping or sight-seeing?" Greg asked, bringing me back to our conversation.

"Either is fine," I said, smiling in what I hoped was a casual way. Playfully grabbing my towel, I jumped up. "But let's get to it! Waikiki awaits!" I yelled, already half way back to the hotel.

That afternoon, as we toured Honolulu, feelings of inadequacy about myself as a woman tormented me. Even though I was struggling to work through the feelings about myself and men, I was still trapped by my weight. Would my feelings be more resolved once I was thin? I was still angry at men, still the victim of the prejudice I experienced. Would it be different when I was thinner, when men finally found me attractive? Would I be more benevolent toward them? My internal dialogue blinded me to the exotic beauty of Hawaii, and I tried hard to act normally with Greg.

My mind couldn't get past the rejection I felt from men. Wasn't a rejection of my body a rejection of all of me? Is it egotistical of me to be affronted because some man isn't attracted to me? How do I settle this in my heart? I can't change the way men are. Am I simply dwelling on it too much? I glaringly saw that I was demanding control, and I knew it was a character defect. Clearly, I couldn't make men think or feel what I wanted, and my desire to control only made me miserable.

Over the next few days my confusion settled, as if God were answering my questions. I learned that my questions about men simply weren't pertinent now and that I'd understand in the future.

Our last night in Hawaii holds a stilled place in my memory as simple and lovely. It was a feather of a moment in time. Greg and I sat on our hotel room balcony at the Kaimana Beach Hotel overlooking Waikiki's shore, a soft, warm breeze fluttering our cotton nightclothes. Floating on the balcony above a magical world, we quietly talked about our lives and dreams. Just us. No outside worries or distractions. Looking at his dear face, I wished it wouldn't be taken from my daily view.

But as the sun rose on Waikiki the next morning, we took a taxi to the airport and separate flights back to the mainland — Greg to Seattle and me to New York.

Only a week later Greg was in New York on business. We met with three literary agents who had expressed interest in his management book. As we finished a meeting with one of them, I realized how my view of myself was changing. Rounding a corner in the lobby of the Grand Hyatt hotel, I came face to face with a full-length image of the two of us in a vast mirror. I put the brakes on my usual reaction of ducking my head when I sensed a mirror nearby, and boldly looked up. In the mirror I saw a clear-eyed woman with her head held high. I liked what I saw, even though I had lost only a small percentage of the weight I needed to lose. I was beginning to like who I was inside, and it shined through. I laughed as I realized that Greg noticed too.

It was a wonderful time for us, mostly because I was in a sound place with myself. I felt so good about myself — separate from Greg and accomplished in my own right — that I was free to let our relationship be what it was and enjoy it. In Hawaii I had felt I must be on guard against the attitudes that went with my illness, attitudes that cropped up all over the place — selfishness, resentment, fear, and egoism. But this time together was more natural. More accepting of my physical self, I wasn't afraid to reach out and hug Greg. I didn't feel as repulsive anymore — to anyone. I found I reached more for everyone these days, not anticipating rejection, and thinking less of myself and more of them. Maybe they need a human touch, too, I thought.

ஃ ஃ ஃ ஃ ஃ

I spent the next couple of weekends taking my Fifth Step, which meant reading aloud to my sponsor all that I had written in my Fourth Step. As I finished the last of my Fifth Step in the plaza of a big Manhattan office building one day, Renee turned to me and asked if I was ready to become a food sponsor. I was petrified at the thought of the responsibility of helping others with their food, but Renee seemed to think I was ready. After the initial terror, I remembered that as a food or Step sponsor, I would only be working for God. All I needed to do was work my program, pray to be of use to God, and be honest with myself and the other individual.

As I took my Sixth and Seventh Steps over the next couple of days, I came to a place in my heart where I was willing to give up my past coping mechanisms and defects, and to ask God to remove them. I felt a new peace as I moved on in the Steps, as though my recovery was less precarious. I was realistic about having to work my program of recovery constantly, but felt utterly grateful that I had been given a way out of my obsession.

Having made a list of people I had harmed in my Eighth Step, I began working on my Ninth Step, actually making amends to those people. It was at this time that I faced my most terrifying financial amends head on. I went to see a tax attorney about what I would need to do to clean up my past with the IRS. I learned after two meetings with her that I could begin to pay back taxes in regular installments. I owed a penalty, of course, but my worst fears of being arrested were diminished. I approached the IRS about setting up a payment plan.

I faced some of my most profound and painful encounters when I went home to visit my family in Colorado in July. I had heard that remarkable shifts in relationships happened during Ninth Step amends. Now, I was about to experience them for myself.

The second morning in Grand Junction, I got up early to go for a walk, but ended up sitting on the end of my parents' bed talking to them. As I explained the process of recovery and the details of the Steps, I arrived at the Ninth Step. "I know I have wronged you both," I said, telling them specifically about the things I was sorry for and how I planned to make amends. I turned to Mother, who lay propped up against the headboard. "I'm so sorry that I've had a condescending attitude toward you over the years, Mom," I said, wondering, as she began to cry, whether I even should have brought it up. My heart wrenched, and I felt for the first time the depth of what I had done to her.

But when she began to speak, I understood why it was important to open up to the people I had wronged. "It's hurt me for so long. I'm glad to hear you understand now how I felt and why I turned to other people for the appreciation I couldn't get from you. They thought I was okay, and that made me feel good," Mother said.

It was one of the first times I really identified with her and felt repentant. My sponsor had said that making amends wasn't just about words but required action. I had to change my attitude in the future. "I truly am sorry, Mother. I feel like you have given me so much and that you do the same for others as well," I said, reaching to hug her. After that, I found I could see the good in her more clearly. The wall of indifference that protected me emotionally had vanished, and I wanted to let her know me.

A few days later, my father drove me to Aspen, a couple of hours away, to join a press group at the Snowmass Club Resort. I felt tense. Something had shifted between me and my parents since I had been so open and vulnerable with them, and Dad was talking now about his own life. "I have really failed you kids in some ways in the past, by working all the time," he said. I smiled, but withdrew inside. I didn't want to hear intimate stuff about his doubts and fears. I wanted to pull away from him, uncomfortable at being that close. He wasn't being "the father"; instead, he wanted to talk about things that were personal and uncertain. Where was the all-knowing, strong father I had put on a pedestal all my life? He was straying far from the image I was familiar with, and it scared me. I was too fearful to see him as another human being with problems, a person I could listen to and maybe even help.

After Dad left me at the hotel that day, I dove into the pillows to weep, and I wasn't sure why. I had tried to concentrate on reading the Big Book, but mostly I slept — dreaming, crying, and staring into space. Food wasn't an option for dealing with my pain.

😿 😿 😿 😿 😿

Once I was back in New York, I found myself trying to hide out and escape with thoughts of travel or men, rather than facing feelings that were unrecognizable and confusing to me. Food cravings started returning — thoughts of the old comfort in Häagen-Dazs and Reese's peanut butter cups. Although I wasn't seriously considering bingeing, I knew it was the next step. Some part of me was denying resentment or fear, a luxury I couldn't afford because it meant I would fall back into my addiction. Renee told me to go back to the moment I began to feel off track, back to where my insides began to unravel, back to Colorado.

The afternoon that I spoke with Renee, I experienced one of the most stark changes in my recovery: I learned a hard lesson about the damage that resentment did in my life. Since that day in Aspen, when I had shut off my feelings with Dad, things had gone downhill. Now, as I sat writing, reviewing my feelings about my interaction with my father, I realized I was terribly angry at Dad for shaking my view of reality. In a matter of minutes, he had shattered my old, rigid view of life by expressing uncertainty about who he was and how he behaved. Dad, who had always been a symbol of strength and complete knowledge for me, had admitted to being fallible, and I was furious at him. But I denied that intense feeling, and because of that, other resentments piled up. Everything from someone being rude to me in a store, to Greg not calling back when he said he would became a cause for resentment. Without food to numb my feelings, the pain got bad enough that some part of my mind was finally forced to open up and work through the confusing and painful feelings.

As I wrote out a Tenth Step about what had happened, I saw how terribly unfair I had been to my father. He had reached out to me for the first time in his life, humbling himself and changing as never before. In response to my new openness, he had done the best he could. I knew I needed to make amends to Dad, so I called him. As I talked to him, I could feel the oppressive feeling in me lift. Sure enough, he had felt uncomfortable with me that day, afraid he had done something wrong. I made him feel that he was less than a good father and was wrong to want to be open with me. Now, as we talked, I opened my heart to him.

That night at my program meeting, I felt spent but serene for the first time in a couple of weeks. I'd faced the truth, and it really was beginning to change my world. Looking at other compulsive overeaters around me, I reached out to them without hesitation or fear of rejection. "Something looks different about you these days, and it's not just the weight loss," my good friend Kyle said. "It's a softness around your eyes." I felt humbled and grateful. I knew that my ability to reach out directly and unself-consciously was a blessing from God. Hours before, I had been only a bite away from relapse.

～ ～ ～ ～ ～

As autumn came to New York, I was taking baby steps toward establishing who I was as a recovering person. One Saturday morning I squarely faced the quandary of learning how to order my day sanely and choose healthy habits. I sat in my apartment wanting to take time to just read or wander the city and was feeling guilty about it. You should be helping someone in the program, doing your Step work, or working on your career, I told myself. Somehow I felt that doing things by myself, such as going to a movie or napping, was a sign that I was sliding back into the illness. Before, they'd always been my escape. But now I wondered if it was okay to just have fun by myself sometimes. I thought back on how I had focused so narrowly on working the Steps these past months, single-mindedly fighting my way out of my addiction.

My mind flipped back and forth, trying to determine what was a healthy life. Since April, unless I was working, helping someone, or spending time with friends, I wasn't sure I was doing what God wanted. I don't have any perspective, I thought, as I got up to do the dishes. I had heard at meetings that God wants us to be happy and that sometimes we have to understand that that means taking care of ourself. But in the past I had abused my leisure time so much, how could

I know that I was now hearing God correctly? How could I know if I was following my desire for escape, or if it was okay to go through an entire day unplanned, doing just what I felt like doing? Too many unplanned days in Hawaii had led me to hiding out from my feelings; my discipline so basic to my recovery. I hadn't felt deprived throughout my recovery because, between working, attending meetings, doing recovery work, and being with people, I had had no time. Was I wrong now to want a day to play?

In the end, I took the afternoon to wander the streets of Manhattan, and I discovered new sides of myself. As I perused the boutiques on Madison Avenue, I realized how much I had to learn about Heidi. I had spent so much of my life trying to learn how to mold myself to be what others wanted that I had never asked myself simple questions about what I liked. Looking in a jewelry store window, I tried to pick out the earrings *I* liked, unencumbered by past ideas of what was appropriate for an overweight woman or what would create a certain impression. I longingly fingered a pair of hiking shorts in another store and felt frustrated: I was recovering on the inside but was still large on the outside, and part of me was impatient to go hiking or be physical.

Throughout the fall I continued making Ninth Step amends, seeing those people I could in person and writing letters or calling those I couldn't. One day in mid-September, when I spent essentially an entire day making amends, I learned to what lengths I was willing to go to recover from compulsive overeating. Three very different interactions gave me a deeper understanding of the healing power of the Steps to recovery that I had been taking. First, I saw Dick Todd, an executive at McGraw-Hill who I had worked with on a committee at church. We had a warm and understanding conversation in his office at the McGraw-Hill building — about how I felt I had let him down in not following through on work with the committee and about my recovery in general. It dashed my ego to break the image I thought he had of me, but we were able to talk openly about God and food addiction. He said he understood, having a little problem with sugar himself.

My serenity turned to wariness as I left Dick's office and took the elevator a few floors down to see Henry Conrad, an editor I had worked with while I was a McGraw-Hill trainee. Of the various editors I planned to make amends to for the time I had stolen by going home to binge and sleep, I most feared facing him. My bubbling exterior had never penetrated his reserve when we had worked together, and I feared that he would receive me cooly now. I stepped off the elevator and asked the receptionist to buzz Henry. I fidgeted with my coat as I considered facing this man whom I had known six years before, and then only for a brief time. It would be hard to tell him my most intimate failings.

Henry's secretary said he was with the publisher, but I could wait in his office. As I sat down in a chair across from the broad desk waiting for him to arrive, I realized that I had had an expectation that we might turn out to be pals, or at least have the same warm interaction I'd had when I'd made other amends. But it wasn't likely, I realized with a sinking feeling. I had to bite the bullet and focus on making the necessary amends.

Even before the meeting began, it was tormenting because there were delays, and we were interrupted by the publisher. During one of the delays, I realized — too late — how selfish I had been in simply showing up without an appointment. This is stupid, Heidi, I thought, wondering how I could correct it. Here I am trying to do things right and my selfishness still comes in. I wanted to do it now, so I just came. Offering to come back would only put him out more, I realized as he rushed in.

"Listen, I'm sorry to just show up like this, Henry," I said nervously. "But I only need five minutes."

Sitting down at his desk, he looked distracted and said, "Good, because that's all I have."

Emotionally pulling up my bootstraps, I realized I was here to make amends, plain and simple. So just do it. "Henry, I'm here to talk to you about how I dealt with you when we worked together. I am a compulsive overeater and in a program of recovery. In order to recover I have to straighten out my past, and that means making amends for wrongs I have done. When I worked for you I didn't do my best, and sometimes when I said I was going to the library I actually left to binge." It all came out in a rush. Looking disoriented, he didn't say anything. "Because I stole time from the magazine and you, I want to apologize and make amends by writing some articles without payment."

Then he spoke. "I only remember it a little, that you weren't there at times." He was civil enough, but I could tell he still had hard feelings. "We don't take work free, and I'm retiring soon anyway," he said simply, pushing his chair back to signal that our conversation was over.

"Well, I wish you well in retirement and thank you for seeing me," I said as I turned and walked out the door, shaking inside until I was out of the building.

As I walked a few blocks to my old apartment where Katherine still lived, I reviewed the past few minutes. All my life I had tried to avoid unpleasant situations, or anything that would provide feedback that didn't agree with my self-image. I tried so hard to control what people thought of me, and in making amends to Henry, I had had to tolerate knowing that he probably thought I was crazy. You did it, Heidi, I said to myself. You didn't back out in fear. I've done my best to fix my wrongs, I thought, with a sense of freedom.

My mind turned then to the amends I would make to Katherine. I realized I had a different sort of fear with her — of letting her get too close to the intimate details of my life, as though she would smother me if she did. What was it I was afraid of? I asked myself. Was it that she'd see too much? Well, I didn't have anything to hide anymore. Was it that I would have to give her something I didn't want to? Well, I'm willing to do whatever God's will is, I told myself. I suddenly realized that if I was relying on God and willing to go into the situation with an open heart, I had nothing to fear. I had to turn my attitude around to helping her and amending my wrongs.

Over lunch I did that. It was amazing how things evolved. I really enjoyed her, and our talk. After I went through my list of specific amends to her, we talked and laughed. I was making amends as much by being there and interacting as by my words. I saw what my sponsor meant when she said the Ninth Step could transform relationships. There wasn't any discomfort between us anymore; rather, our relationship was like an open smile. My attitude had softened my heart tremendously, and I felt a genuine love for her. I felt she was a friend, and I talked about things I never had to anyone else.

🐦 🐦 🐦 🐦 🐦

A few weeks later, a press trip to the U.S. Virgin Islands brought a couple of milestones in my transformation. As I got off the plane I couldn't stop grinning at the memory of how I sat somewhat comfortably between the armrests on the seat. It was amazing to fly without the trauma of fearing that the seat belt wouldn't be long enough or that I would be too big for the seat.

The first night when the public relations woman at the Stouffer Grand Beach Resort told us that we would be snorkeling when we sailed to St. John the next day, my first reaction was elation. Then, looking down at my body, depression hit. I was changing, but I wasn't thin yet. At 250, I weighed only 40 pounds less than I had in Hawaii. As I pulled on my bathing suit later that night, terror rose in me at the thought of others seeing me fat as we snorkeled. But I wanted so much to try. My fat still controls me, I thought, resentful that I still didn't look good in shorts and couldn't snorkel. Your fat doesn't control you, I realized, as I looked at my image. Your pride does. I determined not to make a decision that night, but to trust the day to God and focus on others. I'd see how I felt about it when the time came.

As we sailed toward the island of St. John, I wore my sundress over my swimsuit. Looking out at the shimmering waters, I thought about how only a few months earlier in Hawaii my fear of letting people see me in a swimsuit had stifled my spirit. Overwhelmed with embarrassment then, I had made excuses not to swim. Please help me work through this, I prayed silently now. The fear slid away in minutes, and I didn't worry or anticipate the moment when I would have to make a decision. Ironically, once I had dealt with the fear, I never considered trying to get out of snorkeling. I had hidden behind my body inhibitions for so long that I couldn't remember the last time I had done something physical that was totally new to me.

As we dropped anchor to snorkel, I slipped off my sundress without thinking, grabbed my snorkel gear, and slid off the edge of the boat into the water. The true Heidi came out, leading the pack toward adventure. I was giddy with the thrill of being able to do it. This is me. It always was, I thought. No wonder I had felt so frustrated reining in my exuberance, watching others do what I desperately wanted to. Swimming along with new buddies and holding a maroon sea urchin, I discovered a whole world of senses I had denied myself. I had looked at my body the night before and thought, no way can I do it. But God changed my attitude. I focused outward. I didn't look that much better than in Hawaii, but I was settled inside and with God.

It was funny how the ego deflation worked. By letting down my image, I felt more relaxed and closer to people and more accepted. I guess it was because I accepted myself and didn't need to keep up a pretense of being someone I wasn't.

I became more aware of my body in subsequent months and noticed my body language changing. I'd find myself crossing my legs — which I could do now — and feeling positively leggy. As I walked home with Deborah from *Successful Meetings* one day, I realized how open I was becoming to experiencing new things. I was more welcoming and less fearing of the world.

"So what sports do you want to try?" she asked as we walked along Third Avenue.

Like a kid, I plucked them out of the air. "Tennis, of course. And skiing. Maybe racquetball, squash, and softball." The thought of all the experiences I had never had — of whacking a tennis ball, sliding into home base, or just enjoying running — made my head spin. I felt like I'd been in hibernation or sick, not experiencing the simple things most people took for granted.

෴ ෴ ෴ ෴ ෴

As October arrived, I began to see that what I had thought was the domain of obese women — feeling inadequate and unworthy of love because of my body — was common to many women. Because I had lost almost one hundred pounds by this time, weight seemed to come up in most conversations with friends. Even women I knew only slightly seemed to feel they could confide in me. I was shocked to find that women whom I perceived as thin actually felt fat, or they were inhibited (not just from playing sports but from normal interaction) by some aspect of their anatomy.

One day a good friend said she knew exactly how I felt because she thought she was small-busted and wouldn't wear a bathing suit. Another friend said she felt the same sense of freedom after losing fifteen pounds as I did losing one hundred. Before, she felt ugly and depressed, almost as much an outcast as I had felt at three hundred pounds. When a beautiful model I was sponsoring said she turned down dates because she hated her body, I was flabbergasted.

ﷺ ﷺ ﷺ ﷺ ﷺ

In mid-October, I visited Greg for a week in Seattle. This trip was a revelation for me; it showed me how I presented myself to the world when I was compulsively overeating, and it gave me the opportunity to see the changing Heidi in a new light. My first night there, after an evening out, Greg and I settled on his couch for a frank discussion of my body image when I was fatter. We both laughed when he said I hadn't fooled him by always hiding behind people or striking a certain pose to hide my fat in photographs. He had also noticed my discomfort in chairs and airplane seats. I thought I had hidden it all so well.

As the conversation turned serious, I asked why my weight had never bothered him. He said he always felt my relationship with my body was separate from our relationship, so he'd been able to let it be my problem. "I had a relationship with you, and I figured you had to work out the other on your own," he said.

"But my body *is* me," I responded quickly.

He looked solemnly at me and said, "But it wasn't then." I had to agree. I felt that my body and spirit had become much more unified in the past couple of months.

Before, I had totally separated my spirit from my body. "I noticed the vast mood swings and the total denial of your body," Greg said. "You'd flip from being upbeat and bouncy to being deeply depressed — no middle ground." He'd been almost the only person to see my dark side, but I wondered now if others had experienced my superficial bubbly character as an impenetrable wall.

As I went to bed that night I reflected on the battle I had waged so long with hating my body. Could any man have made it through that battleground and to my soul? I wondered. Now I was beginning to feel whole, female, and attractive; the real me was surfacing and coming together.

The next morning, Greg and I drove east across the mountains to Spokane for a weekend visit with his father. I had decided it was the time for me to make amends to Greg and to face him in an entirely new way. We'd been so honest, but I realized that I had lied to him about things I had been lying to myself about. I had led him and others to believe I'd injured my knee while skiing as a preteen. He was surprised when I told him about the secret bingeing I'd done when we had been together in New York and Vienna. I also told him that I needed to amend my attitude of being subtly pushy and demanding. The hardest thing for me to admit was that I had once read his journal; in my insecurity I had gone through it, looking to see if he had written about other women. He listened, and forgave.

❧ ❧ ❧ ❧ ❧

Soon after I returned from my visit to Greg, my sponsor said it was time for me to stop weighing and measuring my food. At first it scared me. Then I felt like a kid on vacation — for a split second the addicted part of me told me it meant I could eat what I wanted now. But I soon realized that nothing had changed. On my trip to Jamaica the next week, I felt shaky without the security of weighing and measuring my food. I feared the obsession would come back. Praying, I asked for protection from my food obsession. When mealtime came, there always seemed to be enough vegetables to meet my food plan, and I was able to make good choices, eat the amounts I had in the past, and leave the rest. I didn't feel deprived and had no desire to take even a few more bites. God protected me from my obsession: I wasn't fighting food anymore.

Looking down at the numbers on the scale one month after I'd stopped weighing and measuring, I panicked. I'd lost seven pounds. That's a pound less than I've averaged in the last few months, I thought. Suddenly I didn't want to eat anything. I'll skip lunch, just lunch, I rationalized. Picking up the phone, I called Renee. I was clearheaded enough to realize that I should okay skipping lunch with my sponsor.

"Maybe I should cut back on my food so I keep losing as quickly as I have been. I still have at least fifty pounds to lose," I told her.

"Heidi," came her sane voice. "You had some heavier foods in Jamaica, and you still lost seven pounds. Have you tried to find God in your anxiety about losing seven pounds instead of eight? Rely on God to help you make sane food choices." Hanging up the phone, I realized it was the first time in my life that I could imagine being anorexic; it was the first time I had realized that the obsession could flip the other way. Weighing and measuring had been my security, because I knew that if I ate as planned I would lose weight. I sat myself down, breathing deeply. Relax and trust God, I reminded myself. My goal is to eat sanely at each meal; if I do that, weight loss will follow naturally.

By November, with food abstinence and my work in the Twelve Steps progressing well, I realized that recovery meant more than not overeating. I had to be willing to let go of old ways of coping in all areas of my life. One morning I sat reviewing another less-than-perfect article returned from one of my editors. It reminded me of the depth of my fear about finances, and how not relying on God had let that fear run my career — and damage me. Still afraid of not making enough money, I was accepting more assignments than I had time for and then not doing them well.

With a sad heart I realized the problem, which appeared to be about finances and organizing my career, was actually about denying reality. Habits I had learned during my years of hiding out on the couch still haunted me: I didn't want to grow up and take responsibility for my life. All these years I had ignored the future, putting out the biggest fire of the day and eating. It was all I could do to just get by; I never took preventive measures or planned. The moment of truth had to come, I thought. A person can't live on the edge like I have and feel settled. The first step was to pray for the courage to face it all, and the willingness to do what I had to to continue my recovery.

I felt an urgency to fulfill my responsibilities in life and be on the adult course. I had wasted so much time. Pulling out pen and paper, I wrote out how the compulsion to escape had shown itself in my life: procrastinating on taxes, ignoring bills too long, scheduling too many assignments out of fear that I wouldn't have money, not facing that I was powerless over who would and wouldn't assign articles to me, not being able to stick to a budget, and never turning down assignments out of fear the editor wouldn't call again. I was letting the world, and fear, run me rather than discovering God's plan for me and moving methodically in that direction.

I felt antsy, my mind shying away from the fear because the mess seemed too large to handle. How would I ever change attitudes that had ruled my career and financial life for years? I won't think about it right now, I determined as I grabbed a taxi and headed for a press luncheon. Instead, I started obsessively thinking about how Greg didn't appreciate my work on his management book. By the time he called later that evening, I was really angry. Not wanting to come right out with it, I picked at him instead. Hanging up, I realized I was in a funk about my life but it was easier to get angry at Greg and believe my problems were caused by his not doing what I wanted him to.

Suddenly I saw clearly — and was sickened by — my subconscious dance with him. I got what I wanted by manipulating his emotions, creating drama by being deeply depressed or upset. He would then run to my rescue with attention. I got what I wanted by acting in ways that I unconsciously knew he'd respond to. It was unfair and dishonest, I suddenly realized. I could call him back and get reassurance that I was important to him in ways that had nothing to do with the book, but I knew that already. And acting that way isn't me anymore, I thought.

I had always had such an illusion of control in the relationship, believing that I was getting what I wanted. But inside I felt cheated because I knew it hadn't come spontaneously from Greg. I had manipulated it. Now that I saw the truth, I couldn't consciously manipulate him the way I had. My recovery was more important.

Slowly I began to put myself on career and financial abstinence. I admitted I was powerless over how to change the way I had been functioning, and each morning enlisted God's help on the steps I should take to work effectively and pay off some of my debt. I marveled at the miracle of a heart in transition. Praying that the fear would cease, I found myself more willing to let go of the security of past habits, slowly feeling stronger inside.

❧   ❧   ❧   ❧   ❧

As the end of 1987 approached, I came to a profound understanding about my relationship with God. I had always had a relationship with God, but I suddenly realized that it hadn't been one of complete trust. Early in the month of December, my sponsor went into relapse, succumbing to food when she came up against a wall of pain with her husband. Her faith that she would rely on God to help her through it gave way to her relying on her old coping mechanism — eating. When she called to tell me that she wasn't qualified to sponsor me anymore, I felt numb. Fear rippled through me: if she could fall back into the addiction, what about me?

As I was praying a couple of weeks later, I suddenly realized that in some musty corner of my soul, I didn't believe God loved me unconditionally and wanted my happiness. I caught my breath as I sat up out of the kneeling position. I had an image of big, warm loving hands cradling me. But that isn't how I feel, I thought. I can't relax in those hands because I don't feel in my heart that God loves me and wants what will make me happiest.

I thought about all the months I had been in recovery and of my desperate bid to do what I thought God wanted me to do so I wouldn't lose recovery. I had fearfully prayed to be free of selfishness or laziness. That way, I would do what God wanted and expected of me — I could serve God, and the balance sheet wouldn't be weighted too heavily against me. I was terrified that if I wasn't a good girl, God would take away my protection and I would turn back to food. My logical side said that God was kind and loving and wanted me to be happy, but I realized that I had denied the angry corner of my soul that regarded God as a bartering God whose love was conditional. Some part of me sensed that God loved me, but it was crucial that I *feel* it. I prayed to know God's nature and to know in my heart that I was loved.

A few days later a woman in church talked about the deep comfort that she felt had come from God at a moment when she needed it most. It had made her feel that she was on the right track and that God loved her. I cried as I walked home. I wanted that same assurance so profoundly. I prayed, asking God why I didn't have it. Don't I deserve it too? Is it because I demand it? Is that what I'm doing? Or is the truth already in front of me and I can't see it? I wondered. I prayed that at least I would understand why I heard only silence. I felt adrift and abandoned, unsure of my abilities to think and reason. I felt lost, not even knowing what to read or do to fix these confusing feelings. How could I sincerely want to know the truth and be closer to God, and keep missing the mark?

Later that evening I wrote out a Tenth Step on the resentment I had at God for not giving me a flash of lightning or some great sign that God loved me. I realized I had had a tantrum. I had shouted at God, "Show me you love me," looking for a thunderbolt as proof.

Instead, God had whispered, "Look around you."

I had stomped my foot, demanding evidence of unconditional love. But when the storm of anger subsided inside me, the warm feeling of God's quiet assurance of love was there. I laughed at myself, suddenly aware that what I had to do was quit demanding grand gestures and see what was there.

I realized that if I wanted to hear God, then I should draw nearer to him, study his ways, and learn what was expected of me and how the relationship worked. Sitting down, I made a list of the ways God had shown me love in recent months and prayed for my self-pity to be lifted.

That crisis began a period of discovery that I will continue the rest of my life. In the early stages, those next months, I began to define who God was to me from our actual interaction. This became my guide to understanding God's nature; I no longer assumed that God had the same human characteristics as the authority figures I had known in my life. Having experienced conditional love in my family — contingent on whether I was a "good girl" — I had believed that God operated the same way. But when I looked at how God had cared for me even when I was in the depths of my self-centeredness and food obsession, I knew that he didn't care whether I was a good girl or not. God had carried me to a point of recovery regardless of my goodness. I began to see that God loved me for who I was, rather than what I did for him or other people.

On the flight home to Colorado for Christmas I got a powerful reminder of who it was that kept me free of compulsive overeating each day. I looked at the breakfast of an omelette, sausage, juice, and muffin in front of me and realized that I wanted to eat everything. Stopping to pray to know what to eat, I chose the omelette. Then I took a small bite of the muffin. It tasted like cake, and I had a consuming desire to eat it all. Turning to God, I asked that the craving be lifted, and it was. This experience starkly reminded me of how close I always was to compulsive overeating, and it also tipped me off that something must be wrong if I was thinking obsessively about sugary food.

One thing I had learned is that obsessive thinking about food is never about the food. Rather, it's about feelings. Looking inside, I quit denying my feelings and faced the fear that I had about my ability to be home with my family and still maintain my center. My last visit had stirred up many confusing emotions, but it had also taught me a lot, I realized. In general, the moments of flipping back into old fears and resentments had become less frequent. In recent months, I had come to expect less out of every scene and every person, including myself, so I was less often disappointed.

I would do the same at home, I decided. God had been with me during the last visit and had helped me learn what I needed to. He will be with me now, I thought as I looked out the small window of the plane. The words I had heard from the speaker on the weekly broadcast of the Mormon Tabernacle Choir the Sunday before came back to me then. "Trust God enough to throw open your heart to experience. Trust that he knows better than we what will help us grow. Even the dark parts of the stained glass window, stunning and spectacular, are necessary to its whole."

CHAPTER EIGHT

A New Perspective

Winter 1988 — Summer 1989

A smile spread across my face as I opened my eyes New Year's morning 1988 and remembered the past year. It was the first time in my memory that I had wakened on New Year's Day feeling good about the previous year. No sinking feeling inside that another year had passed in which I hadn't changed. I stretched in my bed and ran my hand along my ribs. Yep, they were there. I could feel them. I'd lost 130 pounds in the past year, but it felt as though twice that weight had been lifted off my soul.

In the past the weight was always the symbol of the state my life was in. I'd look down at my body and think of what a failure I had been that year because the fat was still there. But this morning brought no regret over the past, and I was actually looking forward to what 1988 would bring. For once my list of goals wasn't topped by losing weight. As I got out of bed, my thoughts moved on to how different last night's quiet movie with friends had been from the glamour of the year before in Vienna. Much of the evening at the Kaiser Ball at Vienna's Imperial Palace was a blur because I was so consumed with fear, resentment, and the obsession to eat. This morning I didn't feel tense or worried, sure that the lessons God had in store were best for my growth. I had never felt so unsure of what lay ahead, and yet so settled about it.

The next day, as I walked into Macy's department store, my feet automatically took me to the large-size department. After a few minutes of searching, and finding nothing small enough for my size-sixteen frame, I hesitantly moved to the regular-size department. Picking up a skirt, I looked at the salesperson sheepishly and headed for the dressing room. I kept expecting her to come up to me and say, "You're obviously too large to be shopping in this department. Get out."

The skirt fit. My shock turned to exuberance as I moved on to the designer sportswear floor. Picking up a red polka-dot shirt that looked like it would fit, I headed to the dressing room. But there was a green one that caught my eye and a flowered one too. The choices made my head spin. Freedom, I thought as I plucked things off the rack. I couldn't believe that I didn't have to settle for the first thing I found that was cute and fit, as I had to in the past. The idea of browsing — perhaps for days at different stores — before buying was foreign.

I spent hours in the dressing room, pulling on different outfits to discover my style. First a country skirt, then a funky black dress. I grinned, turned sideways, then whirled around. Hmm. Maybe. Pulling on a neon pink-and-orange cropped sweater, I laughed. Was there a shocking side to me? Well, maybe. It was time to step back and think about what *I* liked, instead of what covered my fat or made me look appropriate.

Pulling on a long, slim, black V-necked sweater, I looked up and thought, This is me. A smiling image of a relaxed, confident woman with style stared back at me. I thought of all those women I had admired who pulled on simple classic clothes and ran off to live their lives. They always seemed to have such strong self-images, and lives so busy and full of love, that they didn't bother with faddish clothes. And because of the peace in their souls, their classic clothes expressed who they really were. As I looked in the mirror I cried and laughed, a sense of gratitude and wholeness filling me. I just looked at my reflection in the mirror, thinking how I was beginning to know and love the woman who is me. I was beginning to feel comfortable in my own skin; it was an elusive and precious feeling that I had longed for all my life.

So many friends commented those first weeks of 1988 on how good I looked, that I almost began to forget that the internal healing would be slower to come than the physical healing had. Though I was beginning to look normal on the outside, the years of living as an obese woman caught in a food addiction had taken their toll inside. I had just begun to learn how to deal with people without my shields of fat and food and without having a fantasy life that I could retreat to when the world seemed confusing.

ૐ ૐ ૐ ૐ ૐ

At the end of January, I was confronted with events that would move me into a new phase of recovery. While Greg was in town on business for a week, an old girlfriend of his who had remained a friend flew over from Paris for a few days. With her arrival, I had to face head-on my past fears of being second best and rely on God to show me the truth about my feelings and perceptions. I couldn't be sure which feelings were sparked from the past and which actually existed in my relationship with Greg. I knew I couldn't hide my intense and confused feelings in food anymore; instead, I would have to plow through them.

Marie and Greg had known each other for fourteen years. He still had a few things to settle in his heart concerning the future of their relationship, and I knew I had to respect his privacy to do so. I felt as though it was a time for me to learn how to love unselfishly and let go.

The second evening after Marie arrived, Greg called to ask if I would meet them for drinks. A whirlpool of fear and insecurity threatened to engulf me. I was afraid that she was more important to him than I was, that I wouldn't measure up, that I'd deny my own feelings, and that I was the fool and he didn't care for me. Mostly, my fears weren't based on my relationship with Greg but swirled in from the past. As I walked the few blocks to the restaurant, I prayed for some clarity.

Somewhere along the way an amazing transformation occurred in my heart, and peace and a sane view of things settled over me. I was able to simply focus on being what God would have me be and letting God take care of the rest. The most important thing, I realized, as I took the elevator to the restaurant, is to be true to myself. To be the woman I knew I was becoming. It was an opportunity to prove my gratitude and love to God and to learn to love by putting Greg's needs first in this tough and awkward situation.

For a minute, my heart sank as I approached the table and saw a striking French woman with dark hair to her waist sitting across from Greg. Then Greg's smile drew me in, and he seated me next to him. Greg's sensitivity was subtle but real, as he put his arm around my shoulder or rubbed my back absently as we talked. The calm that had washed over me earlier was almost tangible throughout the next hour. I was feeling an intrinsic confidence that I was beginning to understand came from only one source — God.

Only a few minutes after I walked into my apartment, the phone rang. It was Greg, calling to see if I was okay. To the tune of garbage truck noise — because he was calling from a phone booth on the street — he rushed on about wanting to clarify that he had resolved his past feelings for Marie. He realized that he had been idealizing her for a long time and that a relationship with her would never work. Stopping abruptly, he said he felt really foolish because he was explaining his feelings to me when I hadn't even asked. He seemed anxious to make sure things were right between us. For the first time I felt like the cherished one, the important one. I felt as though I had finally broken through a long chain of negative feelings I had had about my womanliness, desirability, and ability to give and receive love.

Although that next week was difficult, it was important, for the sake of my recovery, to acknowledge long-standing fears that I wouldn't have recognized if Marie hadn't come to town. Greg's visit, though drawing us closer in some ways, showed me that I needed to separate a bit from him emotionally for a while in order to move on with my recovery.

A few nights after Greg left, I came across some old romance novels as I was cleaning my closet. My first reaction was an almost physical revulsion. I plucked one out and gingerly read a few words. The book was so unrealistic and full of fantasy that I felt angry at myself for ever having believed that it was real life. I suddenly saw the fallacy of my expectations of unconditional love, with Greg or anyone. In those books, the hero always wanted the heroine. He never had a bad day when he couldn't face himself, let alone the woman he was involved with. I smiled at the memory of Greg's dedication a few weeks earlier when, sneezing and coughing from a bad flu, he had taken the time to review some ideas with me on an article he knew was important to me. And here I had thought that love was expressed only in passionate, romantic vignettes, not in everyday acts of kindness.

Looking over the books that had formed my perceptions about love, I wondered how these perceptions fit with what I was learning about compulsions. When was love an obsession and an escape from reality, the way food used to be, and when was it a healthy way to draw close to another human being? I didn't want to focus on a relationship with Greg, or any man, to avoid dealing with my fear of being alone and figuring out who I was.

My reverie was interrupted by a call from Greg. "Well, I got Marie off on her flight, and now I'm back in Seattle," he said. At his words about Marie, my old rejection scenario started to kick in. But then something stopped me from buying into it. I don't believe the lie that I'm not good enough, I realized.

I continued to ponder the ramifications of that statement as I got off the phone. There was evidence in Greg's words and actions that I was special to him. So why was I holding on to the rejection scenario? Because if I didn't, then I'd have to let go of my belief in the perfect hero who would sweep me off my feet and make the world wonderful. I'd have to see that Greg had his own needs and human frailties and that love between us wasn't about making my life perfect. I'd have to face a world made of shades of gray. If there isn't one extreme, there isn't the other. Love isn't a wonderful Cinderella fantasy all day long, I realized. It's just two people struggling to learn to love and, at rare moments, touching a bit of the magic. Having to face a real live flesh and blood man, who had past loves and romantic attitudes of his own and who had his own conflicts and fears, was new to me. But he's real, and part of that reality is that he has strong feelings for me, I thought. We have a relationship that is nurturing and good. Very good. Still, I had to mourn the death of my dream a little.

I was learning to live with ambivalence, in myself and others. I'd met a couple of men I was attracted to. At first it confused me, and I wondered if it negated my feelings for Greg. Or was I using my feelings for Greg as a shield, saying I wasn't going to explore other relationships because I was interested in him? I began to pull my focus away from Greg romantically and open my eyes to just enjoying life, meeting new men, and having some fun.

❧ ❧ ❧ ❧ ❧

One night in late February, I took a step that represented my willingness to move into the world of risk-takers and to extend myself physically and emotionally. I went ice skating with a group of friends at Wollman Rink in Central Park. It was my first time on skates since I was a child in Oklahoma City. I pulled on the skates and didn't really consider what I was doing until I stepped onto the ice. Then terror struck. Would my legs support me? Did I have the flexibility and grace to move? Janna, who had skated for years in competition, was at my side. Gentle and supportive, she took my hands like I'd seen parents do with kids earlier, and pulled me along stiff-legged as she skated backwards. Shuffling along at first, I relaxed as she taught me how to glide.

After a few minutes I was able to make it several yards on my own. Looking back at Janna with a sense of triumph, I took another few steps and glided. I did it, I thought as I looked up into the glittering skyline of Manhattan edging the trees of Central Park. I'd taken the risk, and my leg muscles had held me up with a little grace. I hadn't used my body in an organized sport or artistic way in so many years. Step, step, glide — I gave directions to my body, and it responded. I was so proud of myself for having the guts to try something new and for being willing to risk looking like a fool.

The next morning I went shopping for a dress to wear while covering the glamorous party for award winners after the Grammy Awards presentation at Radio City Music Hall for *Successful Meetings* magazine. I didn't own anything vaguely glitzy enough for the black-tie event. As I walked into a store on Fifth Avenue, all I had in mind was a simple, sophisticated — and safe — black silk dress. But there was nothing. When the salesperson brought out a dress of blue spangles and another with bright red beads, my heart fluttered a little. Pulling them on just for fun, I found they didn't look quite right.

"Listen, I've got a beautiful black sequin dress that's perfect for you," she said, rushing out before I could protest. The slinky dress with slits up the side wasn't one I would ever have pulled off the rack, but she insisted I try it. I touched the delicate fluted hem, noticing how the black sequins shimmered with blue and purple lights, and pulled the dress gently over my head. Turning around as she belted it for me, I was startled by the image of a Heidi I had never known before: it was me — except in a dream of "someday" sophistication. I wanted to cry at how beautiful it made me feel. And there they were, my legs. What a discovery. I still felt self-conscious about my knees, feeling they were a little chunky. But, not bad, I said to myself as I moved around in the glittering dress. "I'll take it," I said.

A few days later I walked into the New York Hilton feeling serenely elegant and unafraid of — in fact, even sassily inviting of — male stares. Waiters eyed me as the staff scurried about preparing for the throngs that would soon descend. When the crowds did arrive, I found that I was drawing attention from the tuxedo-clad crew as well. I felt flirty and sexy, chatting first with a fellow from Australia and then a record company executive. It was an amazingly freeing and buoyant sensation.

But the feeling has nothing to do with any man in particular, I thought as I moved away from the conversation and strolled alone down the hall. It's about how I feel about myself. I feel like a different person, or maybe I feel like the real me, I said to myself as I smiled directly into the eyes of people around me. I feel like I'm projecting the image that was inside all along. I *am* growing to like her and feel comfortable with her. I feel more bold and outgoing with men because I feel they aren't going to reject me, I realized.

Branden, one of the men I met the night of the awards, called two days later with an invitation to the Michael Jackson concert that night at Madison Square Garden. He was in film promotion, and a friend had arranged for him to see the show and then stop backstage afterward. I laughed, sure he was kidding because the concert had been sold out for weeks. He wasn't. In a flash, I decided to go for a little excitement. Arriving at the stage door an hour or so later, I met two blonde women. The French one asked, "Are you waiting for Branden?" When I answered yes, she said, "It figures. Branden likes blondes." I reveled in being a part of the scene simply for my looks. That's a new one, I chuckled to myself, as we moved on to other nightclubs.

ﯼ ﯼ ﯼ ﯼ ﯼ

The first of March I took a two-week trip to southern California that combined work and play. The trip brought my emerging body into new territory. After a few days in Los Angeles, where I finished my Ninth Step amends to friends, I joined a press group at La Costa Spa and Resort just north of San Diego. The first afternoon, I researched the spa for an article, feeling uninhibited walking around in a towel and casually dropping it to sit in the Jacuzzi nude.

That night as I slipped on the black sequined dress, a bit of magic came with it. Thirty-one years old, and I had never had the kind of attention that I did that night from men; two handsome, available men simultaneously pursued me rather ardently — mostly just for my looks. They were attracted purely and obviously to my womanly charms. But I knew it was more than my looks. Some key had turned and unlocked something inside me. My enthusiasm at discovering that I could feel at home in my body was contagious. I wasn't shy about smiling or just being myself anymore. Walking into dinner just as the press group was being seated, I was guided by the maître d' to a place next to David, the marketing director for the resort, a good-looking, witty, forty-year-old divorced man. We hit it off immediately, but within a few minutes Stan interrupted from across the table. "I don't believe we've officially met," the bearded, square-jawed free-lance writer said to me. Stan proceeded to recount his recent adventures flying with a fighter pilot to write a magazine article on the lifestyle depicted in the movie *Top Gun*.

This can't be happening to me, I thought as David steered me toward a table in a nightclub an hour later, and Stan showed up on the other side insisting on buying me a drink. Moments later Stan was back with my club soda and an invitation to dance. At first I enjoyed Stan's attention, and the way he was flirting, but then it became intrusive. It was even a little frightening, as I tried to fend off his hands and insinuating remarks as we danced. How do women handle this? I wondered in panic. Did they learn how as teenagers while I was bingeing? I was attracted to him physically at first, but his obnoxious behavior obliterated any chance of my finding out who he was inside. I wasn't sure how to get away from him, and yet in an odd way I was drawn to him because he gave me what I had always wanted from men — validation that I was attractive. Moments later, on the dance floor with David, I felt like a treasure. He softly squeezed my hand, holding me close as we danced slowly.

Part of me felt like a counterfeit as I sat at the table a few minutes later. These men didn't know anything of the former me. What if they knew that a year ago I weighed three hundred pounds? It seemed odd that I could so easily hide my "dirty" past, and I almost felt like I was betraying the old Heidi by not exposing my former obesity. I usually told people about my weight loss, but tonight I just wanted to be who they saw, a carefree, attractive woman without a dark and troubled past.

I suddenly realized that for the rest of my life I would meet people who never knew me before, when I was "fat Heidi." As David gently took my hand, I realized he saw me in a way I didn't perceive myself: I felt like a socially backward little girl, while he and Stan saw an assured woman. As David led me to the dance floor with an appreciative smile, I felt a clutch inside. I was now the heroine in the scenario I had always wanted to be in. It made me want to cry. And it scared me, because I didn't know how to act. Where was the old Heidi?

I didn't realize how deeply my new experiences with men had changed me and my expectations until a week later when Greg arrived for a brief business trip. I was thrilled to see him. We caught up on each other's lives as we took a taxi down to Greenwich Village to see *The Fantastiks,* a long-running romantic musical. As the two romantic leads arrived on stage, my thoughts returned to all the attention I had received from men in recent weeks. Anger, unrecognized until that moment, rose in me. I suddenly realized I was furious with Greg for not making the physical advances that other men had, and for not expressing his appreciation for me as a woman.

The latent, irrational anger that welled up in me occupied my mind as the fanciful musical continued. I sensed that my reaction sprang from a source deeper than Greg's lack of physical interest in me, and as I thought about it, I realized what it was. All my life I had believed that whatever relationship I was in — where the guy wanted only friendship — would be fixed once I lost weight, and then we'd live happily ever after. Now I wanted to have the dream come true. The very fact that Greg had never made demands that I lose weight and become his romantic heroine had drawn me to him initially, but now I was angry. A rejected, obese girl inside of me was demanding, Now that I've lost most of the weight I have to lose, let's get on with things. I wasn't letting things take their natural course, or even considering that Greg might need time to adjust to the changes in me.

By intermission, I was beginning to sort through my ghosts of the past and appreciate the reality of Greg next to me. In the quiet moments, when I thought only of our relationship, I didn't know what I wanted from him. I wanted to relax and just let things happen if they would, but instead a part of me rushed toward love like an exuberant little girl who ends up scaring an exquisite bird with her enthusiasm. I was beginning to understand that love wasn't to be grabbed for, but I still wanted all the experiences that my food addiction and obesity had denied me. In my self-centeredness, I had totally forgotten that Greg had the right to want me simply as a friend.

As we hailed a taxi to head uptown after the show, my mind was preoccupied with questions of romance with strangers and how to be physically comfortable with the man I truly felt emotionally intimate with. I wondered how I could attract other men easily and yet not attract Greg. Was it more complicated than attraction? We had a lot at stake emotionally. My anger was completely gone now, and I was just trying to understand how my mistaken ideas had upset me. As I prayed for my self-centeredness to be lifted and for understanding to come, I felt calm. But there was still an ache inside me as a romantic song came on the radio. I struggled to understand my needs and how to respect Greg's boundaries.

Just then Greg reached for my hand. I curled up next to him with my head on his shoulder as the taxi drove up Park Avenue. It was the quietest solid contact we had yet made — not a quick hug, but just touching and not talking. The pain began to unwind in me: his touch had been so simple, yet it made me feel accepted.

The next night at a movie he took my hand, holding it throughout. It was something new. Our speech had been so intimate at times, but this fragile communication filled a hollow space within me, nurturing me in a new way.

ℛ ℛ ℛ ℛ ℛ

A few months later, one hot July morning in Midtown Manhattan, I sat waiting to begin my work with Alicia, a professional trainer for a project I was doing with *Self* magazine. Sitting in my gym shorts, the first I had ever owned, I thought about the past year. I'd been unconsciously going through the motions of aerobic exercise to stay fit while I lost weight, but now I was going to take a calculated step toward shaping my body. What if I couldn't do it? I wondered. When Alicia showed up, she evaluated my physical fitness and set some goals for me. She then told me that over the next few months she planned to introduce me to different sports that I could add into my current exercise routine. And she was going to set up a routine for me to lift weights, to refine and strengthen my muscles. I can't do that, at least I couldn't before, I thought. I remembered how silly I had felt at times in the past with my obese body in a weight room.

A few minutes later, as I lay on the floor, Alicia moved my legs in various directions as she asked me questions about my body. I became more comfortable and goal oriented as she talked about my body objectively and what I could do to improve different muscle groups. At 192 pounds I had no idea how much more weight I had to lose and was anxious for her to give me precise answers. "I've never been a normal weight as an adult, so I don't know how much I should weigh," I told her. "The weight charts say something like one hundred thirty pounds, but people tell me that I look like I weigh one hundred sixty now. What would I be like at one hundred thirty?"

I listened attentively as she talked about perspective. "You can't go by weight charts. You're five feet, seven inches, but for some reason your long limbs and the way you carry weight makes you look twenty pounds thinner than you are. You'd look emaciated at one hundred thirty pounds. Don't fight it," she finished with a laugh. "Just thank God. Eat healthily and exercise, and your body will settle where it belongs." After that, the actual numbers began to have less of a hold on me.

There were so many little questions I had for Alicia now that I was getting in tune with my body. "I feel off balance when I run for buses, which seems funny to me since I've been working out for a year," I told her as she pulled one of my legs across my body to check for flexibility.

"We'll fix that," she said. "Your center of gravity changes every time you lose ten pounds. No wonder you feel off center, with all the weight you've lost." Moving to lie flat on the floor with me, she taught me how to do scoop sit-ups using the deep smoothing layer of stomach muscle, which flattens the stomach. It was a completely different motion than I had ever done before, and it required me to sense my body deeply and to really feel the muscles engage. Breathing correctly, I sensed a difference as I concentrated on the mental image of scooping that she had explained.

The next week, as Alicia showed me the proper way to work on a Nautilus weight machine, I learned what it meant to consciously combine my spiritual and physical centers. Instead of letting me go through rote motions while pressing the weights, she had me concentrate on the feeling of my muscles as they contracted. As my heart, mind, and body focused, the workout intensified. As soon as my mind wandered, I lost conscious control of my body.

Over the next few weeks, as the deep muscles of my abdomen grew stronger and stabilized my core, I began to discover how crucial my physical, as well as my spiritual, center was to my well-being. For the first time I began to understand the adage that you get out of something what you put into it. I could feel a difference, not just while working out, but in walking more smoothly on the street and feeling more lithe with my flatter stomach.

જ્ઞ *જ્ઞ* *જ્ઞ* *જ્ઞ* *જ્ઞ*

I arrived at my friend Leslie's annual birthday party in September looking chic in a black hat and a close-fitting, short black dress, with a waisted purple jacket and black heels. I look every bit the self-assured sophisticate, I thought as I caught my image in the mirror just inside the door. But I was in turmoil. Over the past week I'd realized more than ever how differently my outside was now compared with before. I was often confused and uncomfortable about it. Just then Leslie introduced me to a friend of hers, saying, "This is Heidi. She just lost over one hundred pounds." Turning to me she added, "I can't even remember what you looked like when you were big and fat."

A few minutes later, after greeting other friends, I found myself sitting on the edge of the bathtub in the bathroom trying to figure out what I was feeling. I knew Leslie's comment was intended as a compliment, but it had stabbed my heart. The hurting little girl inside me still felt the pain of those fat years. It doesn't go away just because the fat has, I thought now. My weight loss seemed public property, and I just wished everyone would forget it. I got sick of people asking me how much weight I had lost. They thought they were complimenting me, but I just felt like a freak.

At the very least, people tactfully commented on how great the new sleek version of Heidi was. But do their accolades mean the other Heidi wasn't okay? I wondered. People really don't know how to react to me now that I come in smaller packaging, I thought wryly. And I didn't know how to react to me either. I could still remember Leslie's party a few years earlier when fear had driven me home to binge after only an hour. I wanted to run now, but there was no food to run to, so I sat in the bathroom.

I didn't know what to think or how to act and desperately wished someone would tell me. Throughout recovery, I had run full tilt from the "other" Heidi. Now I felt schizophrenic — not true to either self — and I couldn't find a middle ground where the two women could meet. All my life I had felt split, the true Heidi locked inside a fat body I despised. Fat, I was the thin woman trying to get out. Thinner, I found myself desperately trying not to deny the fat woman inside who had been me for seventeen years — more than half my life. I was afraid that if I accepted the fat woman, I wouldn't be able to settle into being a normal-sized woman and I would retreat to the old familiarity of being a victim inside a layer of fat. I knew how that felt.

I used to watch pretty, relaxed, and confident women with jealousy. I fantasized being like them and felt that I was that way inside but that nobody else saw it. Now, I projected that assured image and felt it much of the time. But by claiming that image, I sensed I was somehow being a turncoat and felt disloyal to the obese Heidi. I had left her in the dust, without a thought. And now I felt as though I were mourning her death, trying to acknowledge her good parts rather than abandon her completely. What I wanted most was to be a compilation of both Heidis.

As I came out of the bathroom I reached for Kevin, someone who had known me before I had lost weight and who cared about me in a deep way. Putting my arm around his shoulders as he slid his arm around my waist, I felt comfortable and secure as we talked. I needed a human touch to settle my emotions — touch did more to calm me than talking did. I knew that I needed my friends, familiar and unchanging in their reactions, as I pieced together my new perceptions of myself. They won't leave me because friends don't, I thought, as I looked around at them. They are always here. I was amazed at how fragile I felt, disconnected as I was from my former self by all the recent physical changes. When I thought of leaning on any of these people, I knew I could — not in the old way when I expected them to discern my needs, but in the sense that if I honestly expressed my needs, I could count on them to respond. I knew that with them I could be who I really was.

That night I looked at old photographs of myself and felt compassion for that sad obese woman's pain as I began to own her as part of me. I realized I needed to stop and take a deep breath to evaluate the effect of the past year and a half. I'd been in the middle of the process and hadn't looked at what it meant to my life. What happens when you are finally capable of moving toward your dreamed-for image of satisfaction and happiness? I wondered. My reality had shifted along with my perception of my own boundaries and my concept of what was possible for me in this world.

๙ ๙ ๙ ๙ ๙

I want to binge, I realized with a start as I sat in the Nashville airport early in 1989 on my way home from a business trip. Not really binge, but to eat whatever I want. No, I thought, it's bingeing I want. I was scared of those thoughts, but was

I scared enough? I won't binge, I said to myself. Some corner of strength and protection was inside me in spite of the crazy idea of finding escape in food. Instead, I started the head games about what I would or wouldn't eat — abstinently. Despite this flare up of the addiction, I knew my deepest desire was to come through sanely. I'll have peanuts, I thought. No, they have oil, and I've already had my oil allotment for the day. Then, conveniently forgetting about the oil, I got some popcorn. By now I knew I was off. Even as I ate the popcorn I prayed for God's protection in spite of myself.

Is it all too late for me? I wondered. No, it can't be. What would I tell a sponsee if she were in this situation? Read the Big Book. Meditate. Pray. Write. Anything but reach for food. Okay, okay, I will. I looked up at two men across the way eating popcorn. I wanted more. I wanted to stuff it down by the crateful. Anything to stuff the feelings. What feelings? What has got me so anxious that I want to run away?

A hint of feeling came as I started to write. It was a deeper feeling and hard to identify. It was a yearning I had felt when Jordan, a close friend, had hugged and kissed me earlier. As we came out of the meeting room, he had put his arm around my shoulders, squeezed me, and kissed my hair as we walked down the hall. I felt something stir, and it wasn't sexual. Something reverberated inside me from my past. I sensed that the strain of feeling ran much deeper than sexuality. Am I hungry for the physical attention of casual touch? I wondered. For the acceptance of me and my body that's implicit in that? Or am I angry at all those men who couldn't simply put their arm around me in a casual way that said they enjoyed touching me when I was fat? Am I angry at myself for all the years I spent feeling untouchable?

I felt sad as I thought back on the scene with Jordan and compared it with my life as the obese Heidi. Today, I could spontaneously express affection without fear that the recipient would be repulsed. It had been such a wonderful feeling walking down the hall next to Jordan. I had felt womanly; not sexual, necessarily, but feminine. Before, I had denied myself not only the female form but also the feeling of being graceful and acceptable as a woman. Now I was accepting my birthright of being a woman and feeling like one.

Sitting in the airport now, my pen could hardly keep up with the feelings pouring through me. I felt the pain of all the years that I had felt alienated from the human race. I had believed I was untouchable and had always felt like a fraud, without a place as a woman. In recovery I had begun to feel more deserving of my birthright as a woman as I became more generous in spirit. I wanted to hug everyone these days, to make up for lost time and feel how my body was in hugs. My feelings — all sorts of feelings — were much closer to the surface these days too. I felt more genuine love for people as fellow human beings. It was so new, and so odd, this ability to feel deeply. It was more painful than the way I used to live. Maybe that's why I squash it down, I thought. It hurts to not be with people I truly like and it is terribly painful to be apart from those I love.

Then, the food obsession ended. I'd been protected. I'd chosen to feel. I was exhausted as I boarded the flight to New York.

Soon after getting back from Nashville that winter, I went into several months of "terrible twos," resenting that being thinner hadn't delivered all it had promised to in my mind. I still faced all the financial, career, and personal problems I ever had. All my life some part of me had believed that an ideal, easy world was out there waiting for me. All I had to do was lose weight. Now I knew that dealing with my food obsession was only the first step in accepting that the world is much more complex and ambiguous than I had wanted to believe in the years I was escaping and fantasizing. It was a world I wasn't sure I had the skills to cope effectively in. It was work to change my entire orientation to life, and I was angry that life had to be work. I didn't know how to accept responsibility for my life and decisions — I'd been such an expert at shirking it for so long.

What was I to do, faced with this mine field called adulthood? When I was fat I figured nobody expected much of me. I certainly didn't. I was going to do everything *when* I lost weight. Life was so simple then. I didn't have to wonder what my day would be like. It would be framed by my bingeing and remorse. Always the same — obsessively eating or obsessively planning a diet.

In my mind was a rigid grid of how things worked and what feelings were appropriate to feel and what actions were suitable to take. If I hadn't had a clear idea of how I was supposed to feel, I had figured a way not to feel at all. No gray areas: I simply hadn't accepted anything that didn't fit in my framework. Now, simply sitting with ambivalence was torture. My mind wanted to escape to a clear picture of the future for comfort.

In recovery, my fear of feeling powerless had driven me to apply the same rigid formula to working the Twelve Steps. It had been simple: When I had felt fear or resentment, I had done a Tenth Step. Problem? Here's the answer. I had applied the program as if it were a recipe for solving my problems. That had been okay initially. But now, I began to feel emotions so deep they couldn't be cleared up by the time I went to bed. As upsetting as the first year or so of recovery had been, it had felt like familiar emotional ground. Now I began to come into feelings I truly didn't recognize, feeling conflicting emotions about events and people. It was extremely disorienting.

ↄ ↄ ↄ ↄ ↄ

Life isn't any different, I'm just thinner, I thought angrily one afternoon in April as I walked home from my office at *Successful Meetings*. That isn't true, I realized, looking up at the flawless azure sky visible through new, pale green leaves. When I relied on God there was a vast difference. I thought back over the past twenty-four hours. The night before I'd enjoyed an evening with myself, simply reading and writing in my journal. As I wrote in my journal I had realized that my joy seemed to come from the simple pleasures of the day, such as being with friends, or having the sensation of authentic tiredness that came with a good workout, or knowing I truly had done my best on an article.

But mostly the difference was the serenity inside that enabled me to cope better. In my prayers that morning I had enjoyed talking to God and felt as if God was truly interested in my life. I'd had no desire to isolate myself or escape all day. When I'm in tune with my spiritual center, I know I can rely on God to show me how to feel through all my emotions. With God's help I can accept life's trials as a matter of course, I thought as I sat for a moment on a park bench. I feel unafraid and open to new experiences. Sitting there, aware of the beauty of the park around me and the serenity and gratitude within me, I began to feel that I might be leaving my "terrible twos" behind.

I began to give up a bit of my death grip on controlling my environment the weekend my cousin Lana came to visit from Los Angeles. We spent most of the time kicking around the city with a couple, Peter and Melinda, who were good friends of ours. As I talked to Melinda on the phone the first morning of Lana's visit, I felt antsy. I wanted to nail down our plans for the day, but she suggested we play it by ear. "Let's just wander around Midtown poking in shops, and later if we want we'll take Lana to the Empire State Building," Melinda said casually.

What would I say to these people for hours on end? I wondered as I got off the phone. Could I relax? I wasn't used to just hanging out with people other than Greg and I was uncomfortable with not having a clear idea in my mind of how the interaction would go. I could control an evening, picturing a movie and then a couple of hours of conversation over dinner. The thought of several unplanned hours, however, made me nervous. But these are good friends, I thought as I walked up to where the three stood smiling in front of Bloomingdales. It felt risky to just show up for life that day and see where it took me.

As we stood in a chic little hat shop in the Trump Tower a couple of hours later, I watched Lana and Melinda, two beautiful blondes, trying on hats. It was a store I would never have entered before. Too many mirrors. As I watched their reflections, I caught sight of my own animated face next to their faces. Looking back again, I smiled. How about that? I fit right in with them.

Just then Lana picked up a broad-brimmed fuchsia hat and handed it to me. "Heidi, why don't you try it on?" she asked. Novel idea, I thought. I was so used to watching life, it never occurred to me to jump in and have fun. I never thought I deserved to be in there playing.

"Well, why not?" I responded, putting on the sophisticated hat and hiking it back on my head.

"No, no," Melinda said, coming over to adjust it. "Pull it down over the brow. There, it gives you some mystery." It looked entirely different — and so did I.

❧ ❧ ❧ ❧ ❧

Two events the next week made me realize I'd crossed a threshold and was ready to reach out to other humans and become vulnerable in ways I never had before. Tuesday was a horrible day, consumed with articles to finish and financial pressure. I was emotionally on edge, but didn't know what to do about it. Do the laundry? Clean the apartment? Go to a program meeting? I paced instead. Then picking up the phone, I dialed Victoria's number at the office where she worked. As a good friend also in recovery, she would understand. But after a brief conversation in which I casually asked her if she was going to a program meeting that night and listened to how she was doing, I hung up feeling cheated.

Why don't people ever listen to me? I thought as I went to the kitchen to start dinner. I'm so sick of being the listener. I felt wronged and martyred, but mostly just alone and frightened. Some part of me understood there was something I was doing to myself that kept me from being nurtured, but what? Jerky sobs shook me, stilling my hand as it stirred the soup I was warming. "I don't know how to act differently," I said to the empty room as my mind tried to link onto something that made sense. "Please, show me a different way," I prayed. Sitting on the couch, I thought of calling Victoria back. But if I'm going to call her I need to make sense of what's wrong with me so I can explain. But I don't know what's wrong with me. I realized that a deep part of me always felt like there was something wrong with just expressing incoherent emotion. I always had to justify my emotions.

At that moment I determined to break the cycle. I didn't know what I would say to Victoria, but this time would be different. "I just had to call back and be honest with you about how I feel," I said shakily when she answered the phone. I let loose a barrage of fear and anger at how hard the week had been and at how uncertain my life was at the moment. After a few minutes, my crying and talking wound down. I felt a release.

"I'm really glad that you broke the pattern tonight by reaching out and taking a risk," she said. "I thought you sounded upset, but you kept saying you were fine."

"I protect that image of perfect, uncomplicated recovery so much," I said, "because I think I have to be perfect. I'm so afraid of letting people see me out of control, so sure that they'll judge me."

When I hung up, I realized how good it felt to have taken a risk with Victoria, to see that I was worthy of her taking time for me. I had never reached out to her — or anyone — in a moment of serious emotional crisis. I was always there for her and never begrudged it, but somehow I didn't think she would want to be there for me.

That night I stayed home and spent time with myself, doing the daily tasks that felt comforting now that I was in touch with my feelings. But the next night I realized I truly needed to reach out to the fellowship of the Twelve Step program. I'd been working on an article and couldn't make sense of it, so I took a break and walked a dozen blocks south to the old stone church where many of the meetings were held.

I wanted to speak in the meeting, but couldn't summon the usual positive recovery comments. I had a heartfelt need to share my pain and uncertainty in recovery and to know that others had experienced the same. It was a large meeting, so my raised hand got lost in the crowd. At the end of the meeting the leader asked if there was anyone who really needed to share. My first thought was that someone else probably needs it more than I do. In my hesitation the leader called on someone else. Then, breaking the rule of going over the time, the leader turned to me because he'd seen my hand. It was a humbling moment as I shared my fears about losing weight and handling feelings that I had always binged my way through before. For the first time in a meeting I cried, and it was okay. Afterward, as people came up and hugged me, I felt resounding support. I could let the love in and let down my pride and image.

After that I seemed able to share other emotions more readily, telling a public relations person who called after 6:00 p.m. on Friday that I was off duty and asking her to call back on Monday, and expressing my anger to an editor about how one of my articles had been changed.

One June afternoon several weeks later I said one last good-bye to Deborah, an editor at *Successful Meetings,* as she finished packing boxes for a move to Boston with her fiancé. Hanging up the phone, I started to cry, realizing how much I would miss her. She had been a true friend throughout my recovery, a time when I so needed one. Such friends are rare, I thought. We laughed at similar things and faced similar problems, instinctively understanding each other. She was one of my first really close female friends. We were friends in a healthy way — we gave and received equally.

That evening as I went for a walk, I felt so blessed to be able to love people and to feel sadness, because it meant I could also feel happiness. I had pushed *all* the feelings down before, living in my self-contained capsule. Sighing, I realized that fundamentally I was very satisfied with my life. I felt sad at the moment, but was relaxed in my sadness because I could just feel it rather than frantically run away from it through food or activity. I could, because I wasn't carrying it alone. God was there to ease the pain and help me grow in the way I wanted to. There was such a fine line between letting go and feeling in an honest way, and falling into depression, but I was beginning to learn it. Part of it was recognizing that I wasn't a victim and seeing how blessed I was.

Yes, I was content, but I knew I wanted more. I didn't desperately need Greg, or any man. Yet, I thought my life would be richer by sharing intimacy and camaraderie with someone. I didn't know whether it would be Greg, but I felt ready to find it with someone in God's time. It had come time in my recovery to recognize this want and to turn it over to God.

Through the next few months I had many new experiences that delighted me. But there was also the sweetness of returning to places inside myself that had long been denied. One afternoon as I waited for Victoria, I couldn't take my eyes off the piano in her living room. Though I hadn't played in years, the memory of how much I had liked to play tugged at me, and I sat down on the piano bench. Picking out the melody of John Denver's "Sunshine On My Shoulders" felt uncertain at first, but became familiar. It isn't a flawless rendition, but you can recognize it, I thought. It's one more tiny step back to the old Heidi.

I suddenly realized what I was saying. All these months I'd thought of the old Heidi as obese and sad and wondered who the new Heidi was, yet here I was discovering the essence of the old Heidi — the exuberant, open child I'd lost. The food addiction had not only silenced the piano, stilled the horses' hooves, and halted the pirouette in front of the ballet mirror, but had stolen the security of trusting myself and the world around me. The Heidi I grew to despise and regret was not the heart of me — rather a woman who had withdrawn to become an isolated shadow. Turning from the piano, I realized that the new Heidi was shedding not only physical weight, but a heaviness of sorrow that weighted my spirit as well. I was returning to the me who had been squashed by the pounds in later years.

❀ ❀ ❀ ❀ ❀

Two months later, as the meadows of the Rocky Mountains were awash with late summer wildflowers, I flew to Colorado to write an article about a dude ranch. I awoke at five the first morning, like a kid on the first day of camp. In five hours I'll be riding a horse, I thought as I jumped out of bed and tried to figure out what to do with the time. Butterflies of excitement filled my stomach. This day had been in the back of my mind since I had started to recover. It had been twelve years since the day when Loren had shattered my world by saying I couldn't ride until I lost weight. Now, I was returning full circle, only to a better place. I had dreamt of riding as I slept the night before, going through the process of getting on the horse and holding the reins as I remembered. I was still afraid that I was too heavy and would hurt the horse.

The sky was just brightening over the mountains when I decided to go for a walk before having breakfast with the public relations woman from the resort. Coming out of my room, I bent to my familiar stretching position and then began walking, picking up my pace quickly. Hopping over a boulder and walking along a fallen tree trunk as though it were a tightrope, I headed toward an airstrip that ran along the edge of a small lake. As I reached the far end of the airstrip I spotted an inviting grassy hillside. Grinning gleefully, I lengthened my stride and ran as hard as I could up the hill. Ta, da. I did it, I thought, laughing out loud, enjoying the sensation of sweating and breathing hard. The warm glow of my working muscles spread through me.

Stopping for a moment, I breathed in the crisp morning air as my eyes drank in the meadows that spread to the dramatic stone mountains in the distance. I thought of a story a friend had told me a few weeks earlier. As a child he took walks with his father through fields in Idaho. Running along while holding the strength of his father's hand, he would half run and half fly. That's how I feel these days, I thought, laughing to myself. Sometimes I can't catch my breath between life's lessons. God is teaching me a lot about living in the moment and having faith. But if I hold on tight, buoyed by God's strength, sometimes I feel as if I'm flying. How exhilarating and frightening it feels, but I don't feel alone, I thought as I headed back down to the airstrip in my solitary workout.

After breakfast, I tried to contain my enthusiasm as the others arrived for the trail ride. I poked my head into the tack room to talk to Joe, the ranch hand, and was overcome by the memory-laden smell of leather. "Can I help?" I asked, too excited to sit still. "I used to ride a lot. I could put the bridles on the horses for you, or saddle them."

Joe slowly raised his head. "Nah. I can handle it," he said. Watching as he saddled the five horses, I wondered which one would be mine and mentally calculated whether I could get up on the saddle without help. What if I can't get on alone because of my left knee not being strong enough? I worried. Images of my riding days of twelve years earlier came to mind. Loren had led my horse alongside a ledge so I could get on while the others in the class looked on, or worse, he sometimes put his shoulder against my rear and heaved me on. Even now I blushed in embarrassment.

Finally we were ready, and Joe pointed me toward a quiet palomino gelding named Charlie. Slipping my left foot into the stirrup, I checked to see if anyone was watching and held the saddle horn tightly while I prayed that I could get on unobtrusively. Then, with a deep breath, I pulled myself up. I was on top before I knew it; my muscles and smaller body carried me faster than I had anticipated.

As we arrived in a mountain meadow a half hour later, the group stopped to watch a doe a few yards away. She perked up, eying us keenly. Then, hop, hop and she was to the far side of the meadow. Something stirred in me, a memory of this morning when I'd run through the meadows with agility, too, and a memory of riding long ago and feeling a kinship with earth, animals, and sky.

I lingered, smiling to myself, as the group moved on. As my eyes drifted to the ground nearby, I caught sight of my shadow — long and lean above the horse. It was then I realized that I was being transformed. I've spent the first thirty years of my life in a world of incorrect attitudes that made me very unhappy, I thought. But, I'm peeling away the layers and returning to my true heart, a heart close to God.

Feathery clouds stretched across the endless horizon as a joyful, soulful prayer of gratitude escaped my heart. The opportunities ahead of me seemed as endless and promising as that horizon. Simultaneously laughing and crying, I turned my face to the sky and thanked God. I had come home to my heart and soul.

THE TWELVE STEPS OF ALCOHOLICS ANONYMOUS*

1. We admitted we were powerless over alcohol—that our lives had become unmanageable.

2. Came to believe that a Power greater than ourselves could restore us to sanity.

3. Made a decision to turn our will and our lives over to the care of God *as we understood him.*

4. Made a searching and fearless moral inventory of ourselves.

5. Admitted to God, to ourselves, and to another human being the exact nature of our wrongs.

6. Were entirely ready to have God remove all these defects of character.

7. Humbly asked Him to remove our shortcomings.

8. Made a list of all persons we had harmed, and became willing to make amends to them all.

9. Made direct amends to such people wherever possible, except when to do so would injure them or others.

10. Continued to take personal inventory and when we were wrong promptly admitted it.

11. Sought through prayer and meditation to improve our conscious contact with God *as we understood Him,* praying only for knowledge of His will for us and the power to carry that out.

12. Having had a spiritual awakening as the result of these steps, we tried to carry this message to alcoholics, and to practice these principles in all our affairs.

---

*The Twelve Steps of A.A. are taken from *Alcoholics Anonymous,* 3rd ed., published by A.A. World Services, Inc., New York, N.Y., 59-60. Reprinted with permission.

Other titles that will interest you . . .

Inner Harvest
Daily Meditations for Recovery from Eating Disorders
  Meditations from the author of *Food for Thought* for those of us who are moving along in our recovery from anorexia, bulimia, or compulsive overeating. Each reading helps us develop self-acceptance, spiritual awareness, and courage. 400 pp.
Order No. 5071

Listen to the Hunger
  Hunger can reflect a number of unsatisfied needs, and mask anger, fear, loneliness, fatigue, or boredom. This book teaches us how to listen to the wisdom of our inner voice to discover what's really behind our craving for food. 71 pp.
Order No. 5008

Abstinence in Action
Food Planning for Compulsive Eaters
  by Barbara McFarland and Anne Marie Erb
  Build self-esteem by developing a personal plan for recovering from compulsive eating. The easy worksheets, structured activities, nutritional facts, and basic explanations in this book will help us develop an individual food and exercise program to structure our daily eating needs. 140 pp.
Order No. 5045
